The Imitation of Christ of Thomas à Kempis (Annotated)

Translator By William Benham

Historic context

This book has a set of temporal, social and cultural circumstances that surround the events, and that may be relevant to better understand its content.

There are many examples in which historical events have shaped the contents and forms of literature, as well as this has on many occasions been the best testimony of the importance of certain events throughout history.

In this case, data such as those related to the author, the time and the place where it was written will be indicated. In the same way, its meaning will be determined and it will expose both the distant and the close antecedents of said work.

The Imitation of Christ of Thomas à Kempis by William Benham
The Imitation of Christ a is a book of Catholic devotion and asceticism written in the form of brief councils whose objective, according to the text itself, is "to instruct the soul in Christian perfection, proposing Jesus Christ himself as a model", according to the school from the modern devotio The book is also known simply as Kempis, Contemptus mundi ("contempt for the world"), derived from the title of the first chapter of the work, or Booklet of the reform of man. It is considered one of the most influential Christian books after the Bible and with the largest number of readers, making it a classic of mystical literature.

It was first published anonymously in 1418 by some authors and in 1427 by others Throughout history, its authorship has been granted to various religious writers, such as Innocent III, Saint Bonaventure, Henry of Kalkar, Juan de Kempis , Walter Hilton and Juan Gerson, although most of the current scholars agree in considering Tomás de Kempis, member of the congregation of the Brothers of life in common, as their most probable author.

The work is divided into four parts: "Useful notices for spiritual life", "Notices related to spiritual things", "Of inner consolation" and "Of the Blessed Sacrament". In all the chapters the need for interior life and withdrawal from the outside world is emphasized, as well as the importance of the Eucharist and its devotion as the center of Christian life, a belief that would be answered by various Protestant movements that arose at the same time. .

William Benham (1831–1910) was an English ecclesiastic, academic, and author.

Born on January 15, 1831 in West Meon in Hampshire, where his father James Benham was a postmaster, he was educated at the village school. Its founder, the rector Henry Vincent Bayley, made him his secretary, taught him Greek and Latin, and at his death left instructions that the child's education should continue.

Benham was sent in 1844 to St. Mark's College, Chelsea, recently established under Derwent Coleridge, to be trained as a school teacher. Upon completion of his course, he taught in a rural school and was tutor to John Sebright between 1849 and 1852. With the support of the Bayley family, he was able to attend the theology department of King's College, London, where his religious position was influenced by FD Maurice.

In 1857, Benham was ordained a deacon and a priest in 1858. He was appointed tutor and professor of divinity in English literature at St. Mark's, Chelsea, still under Coleridge. He remained there until in 1865 he became editorial secretary of the Society for the Promotion of Christian Knowledge. At the same time, she participated in Sunday's ministerial work as priest of St. Lawrence Jewry, under Benjamin Morgan Cowie. From 1866 to 1871 he was also professor of modern history at Queen's College, Harley Street, in succession to Maurice.

Benham's preaching attracted the attention of Archbishop Charles Longley, who in 1867 made him the first vicar of his local Addington parish, where the archbishop resided. Longley was in poor health: Benham acted as his private secretary during the period of the first Lambeth Conference in 1867, and was with him upon his death in 1868. Longley's successor, Archibald Campbell Tait, awarded him the BD degree of Lambeth made him one of the six Canterbury preachers, and in 1872 he was given the Margate Vicarage.

In Margate, Benham restored the parish church and was president of the city's first school board. In 1880 Tait made him vicar of Marden and in 1882 he was appointed rector of Saint Edmund King with Saint Nicholas Acons,

Lombard Street, a post he held for life. In 1888, Archbishop Edward White Benson made him honorary canon of Canterbury, and in 1898 the University of Hartford, USA. UU., It granted the degree to him of DD. He was Boyle's teacher in 1897 and rural dean of East City from 1903 until his death.

Benham died of heart failure on July 30, 1910 and was buried in Addington.

Benham was a prolific writer. Archbishop Tait's life (1891), with Randall Davidson, was the main work of his later life. He also edited the memoirs of Catherine and Craufurd Tait, the archbishop's wife and son (1879; summary edition. 1882).

Benham produced an edition of William Cowper's poetry in 1870; published in 1873 Companion to the Lectionary (new edition 1884); and translated The Imitation of Christ (1874; new ed. 1905). He edited the reprint series Ancient and Modern Library of Theological Literature. Lombard Street in Lent (1894), speeches by various preachers, presented the kind of sermon that he thought a city church should supply to attract businessmen.

INTRODUCTORY NOTE

The treatise "Of the Imitation of Christ" appears to have been originally written in Latin early in the fifteenth century. Its exact date and its authorship are still a matter of debate. Manuscripts of the Latin version survive in considerable numbers all over Western Europe, and they, with the vast list of translations and of printed editions, testify to its almost unparalleled popularity. One scribe attributes it to St. Bernard of Clairvaux; but the fact that it contains a quotation from St. Francis of Assisi, who was born thirty years after the death of St. Bernard, disposes of this theory. In England there exist many manuscripts of the first three books, called "Musica Ecclesiastica," frequently ascribed to the English mystic Walter Hilton. But Hilton seems to have died in 1395, and there is no evidence of the existence of the work before 1400. Many manuscripts scattered throughout Europe ascribe the book to Jean le Charlier de Gerson, the great Chancellor of the University of Paris, who was a leading figure in the Church in the earlier part of the fifteenth century. The most probable author, however, especially when the internal evidence is considered, is Thomas Haemmerlein, known also as Thomas a Kempis, from his native town of Kempen, near the Rhine, about forty miles north of Cologne. Haemmerlein, who was born in 1379 or 1380, was a member of the order of the Brothers of Common Life, and spent the last seventy years of his life at Mount St. Agnes, a monastery of Augustinian canons in the diocese of Utrecht. Here he died on July 26, 1471, after an uneventful life spent in copying manuscripts, reading, and composing, and in the peaceful routine of monastic piety.

With the exception of the Bible, no Christian writing has had so wide a vogue or so sustained a popularity as this. And yet, in one sense, it is hardly an original work at all. Its structure it owes largely to the writings of the medieval mystics, and its ideas and phrases are a mosaic from the Bible and the Fathers of the early Church. But these elements are interwoven with such delicate skill and a religious feeling at once so ardent and so sound, that it promises to remain, what it has been for five hundred years, the supreme call and guide to spiritual aspiration.

THE IMITATION OF CHRIST

THE FIRST BOOK

ADMONITIONS PROFITABLE FOR THE SPIRITUAL LIFE

CHAPTER I

Of the imitation of Christ, and of contempt of the world and all its vanities

He that followeth me shall not walk in darkness,(1) saith the Lord. These are the words of Christ; and they teach us how far we must imitate His life and character, if we seek true illumination, and deliverance from all blindness of heart. Let it be our most earnest study, therefore, to dwell upon the life of Jesus Christ.

2. His teaching surpasseth all teaching of holy men, and such as have His Spirit find therein the hidden manna.(2) But there are many who, though they frequently hear the Gospel, yet feel but little longing after it, because they have not the mind of Christ. He, therefore, that will fully and with true wisdom understand the words of Christ, let him strive to conform his whole life to that mind of Christ.

3. What doth it profit thee to enter into deep discussion concerning the Holy Trinity, if thou lack humility, and be thus displeasing to the Trinity? For verily it is not deep words that make a man holy and upright; it is a good life which maketh a man dear to God. I had rather feel contrition than be skilful in the

definition thereof. If thou knewest the whole Bible, and the sayings of all the philosophers, what should all this profit thee without the love and grace of God? Vanity of vanities, all is vanity, save to love God, and Him only to serve. That is the highest wisdom, to cast the world behind us, and to reach forward to the heavenly kingdom.

4. It is vanity then to seek after, and to trust in, the riches that shall perish. It is vanity, too, to covet honours, and to lift up ourselves on high. It is vanity to follow the desires of the flesh and be led by them, for this shall bring misery at the last. It is vanity to desire a long life, and to have little care for a good life. It is vanity to take thought only for the life which now is, and not to look forward to the things which shall be hereafter. It is vanity to love that which quickly passeth away, and not to hasten where eternal joy abideth.

5. Be ofttimes mindful of the saying,(3) The eye is not satisfied with seeing, nor the ear with hearing. Strive, therefore, to turn away thy heart from the love of the things that are seen, and to set it upon the things that are not seen. For they who follow after their own fleshly lusts, defile the conscience, and destroy the grace of God.

(1) John viii. 12.   (2) Revelations ii. 17.
(3) Ecclesiastes i. 8.

CHAPTER II

Of thinking humbly of oneself

There is naturally in every man a desire to know, but what profiteth knowledge without the fear of God? Better of a surety is a lowly peasant who serveth God, than a proud philosopher who watcheth the stars and neglecteth the knowledge of himself. He who knoweth himself well is vile in his own sight; neither regardeth he the praises of men. If I knew all the things that are in the world, and were not in charity, what should it help me before God, who is to judge me according to my deeds?

2. Rest from inordinate desire of knowledge, for therein is found much distraction and deceit. Those who have knowledge desire to appear learned, and to be called wise. Many things there are to know which profiteth little or nothing to the soul. And foolish out of measure is he who attendeth upon other things rather than those which serve to his soul's health. Many words satisfy not the soul, but a good life refresheth the mind, and a pure conscience giveth great confidence towards God.

3. The greater and more complete thy knowledge, the more severely shalt thou be judged, unless thou hast lived holily. Therefore be not lifted up by any skill or knowledge that thou hast; but rather fear concerning the knowledge which is given to thee. If it seemeth to thee that thou knowest many things, and understandest them well, know also that there are many more things which thou knowest not. Be not high-minded, but rather confess thine ignorance. Why desirest thou to lift thyself above another, when there are found many more learned and more skilled in the Scripture than thou? If thou wilt know and learn anything with profit, love to be thyself unknown and to be counted for nothing.

4. That is the highest and most profitable lesson, when a man truly knoweth and judgeth lowly of himself. To account nothing of one's self, and to think always kindly and highly of others, this is great and perfect wisdom. Even shouldest thou see thy neighbor sin openly or grievously, yet thou oughtest not to reckon thyself better than he, for thou knowest not how long thou shalt keep thine integrity. All of us are weak and frail; hold thou no man more frail than thyself.

CHAPTER III

Of the knowledge of truth

Happy is the man whom Truth by itself doth teach, not by figures and transient words, but as it is in itself.(1) Our own judgment and feelings often deceive us, and we discern but little of the truth. What doth it profit to argue about hidden and dark things, concerning which we shall not be even reproved in the judgment, because we knew them not? Oh, grievous folly, to neglect the things which are profitable and necessary, and to give our minds to things which are curious and hurtful! Having eyes, we see not.

2. And what have we to do with talk about genus and species! He to whom the Eternal Word speaketh is free from multiplied questionings. From this One Word are all things, and all things speak of Him; and this is the Beginning which also speaketh unto us.(2) No man without Him understandeth or rightly judgeth. The man to whom all things are one, who bringeth all things to one, who seeth all things in one, he is able to remain steadfast of spirit, and at rest in God. O God, who art the Truth, make me one with Thee in everlasting love. It wearieth me oftentimes to read and listen to many things; in Thee is all that I wish for and desire. Let all the doctors hold their peace; let all creation keep silence before Thee: speak Thou alone to me.

3. The more a man hath unity and simplicity in himself, the more things and the deeper things he understandeth; and that without labour, because he receiveth the light of understanding from above. The spirit which is pure, sincere, and steadfast, is not distracted though it hath many works to do, because it doth all things to the honour of God, and striveth to be free from all thoughts of self-seeking. Who is so full of hindrance and annoyance to thee as thine own undisciplined heart? A man who is good and devout arrangeth beforehand within his own heart the works which he hath to do abroad; and so is not drawn away by the desires of his evil will, but subjecteth everything to the judgment of right reason. Who hath a harder battle to fight than he who striveth for self-mastery? And this should be our endeavour, even to master self, and thus daily to grow stronger than self, and go on unto perfection.

4. All perfection hath some imperfection joined to it in this life, and all our power of sight is not without some darkness. A lowly knowledge of thyself is a surer way to God than the deep searching of man's learning. Not that learning is to be blamed, nor the taking account of anything that is good; but a good conscience and a holy life is better than all. And because many seek knowledge rather than good living, therefore they go astray,

and bear little or no fruit.

5. O if they would give that diligence to the rooting out of vice and the planting of virtue which they give unto vain questionings: there had not been so many evil doings and stumbling-blocks among the laity, nor such ill living among houses of religion. Of a surety, at the Day of Judgment it will be demanded of us, not what we have read, but what we have done; not how well we have spoken, but how holily we have lived. Tell me, where now are all those masters and teachers, whom thou knewest well, whilst they were yet with you, and flourished in learning? Their stalls are now filled by others, who perhaps never have one thought concerning them. Whilst they lived they seemed to be somewhat, but now no one speaks of them.

6. Oh how quickly passeth the glory of the world away! Would that their life and knowledge had agreed together! For then would they have read and inquired unto good purpose. How many perish through empty learning in this world, who care little for serving God. And because they love to be great more than to be humble, therefore they "have become vain in their imaginations." He only is truly great, who hath great charity. He is truly great who deemeth himself small, and counteth all height of honour as nothing. He is the truly wise man, who counteth all earthly things as dung that he may win Christ. And he is the truly learned man, who doeth the will of God, and forsaketh his own will.

(1) Psalm xciv. 12; Numbers xii. 8.   (2) John viii. 25 (Vulg.).

CHAPTER IV

Of prudence in action

We must not trust every word of others or feeling within ourselves, but cautiously and patiently try the matter, whether it be of God. Unhappily we are so weak that we find it easier to believe and speak evil of others, rather than good. But they that are perfect, do not give ready heed to every news-bearer, for they know man's weakness that it is prone to evil and unstable in words.

2. This is great wisdom, not to be hasty in action, or stubborn in our own opinions. A part of this wisdom also is not to believe every word we hear, nor to tell others all that we hear, even though we believe it. Take counsel with a man who is wise and of a good conscience; and seek to be instructed by one better than thyself, rather than to follow thine own inventions. A good life maketh a man wise toward God, and giveth him experience in many things. The more humble a man is in himself, and the more obedient towards God, the wiser will he be in all things, and the more shall his soul be at peace.

CHAPTER V

Of the reading of Holy Scriptures

It is Truth which we must look for in Holy Writ, not cunning of words. All Scripture ought to be read in the spirit in which it was written. We must rather seek for what is profitable in Scripture, than for what ministereth to subtlety in discourse. Therefore we ought to read books which are devotional and simple, as well as those which are deep and difficult. And let not the weight of the writer be a stumbling-block to thee, whether he be of little or much learning, but let the love of the pure Truth draw thee to read. Ask not, who hath said this or that, but look to what he says.

2. Men pass away, but the truth of the Lord endureth for ever. Without respect of persons God speaketh to us in divers manners. Our own curiosity often hindereth us in the reading of holy writings, when we seek to understand and discuss, where we should pass simply on. If thou wouldst profit by thy reading, read humbly, simply, honestly, and not desiring to win a character for learning. Ask freely, and hear in silence the words of holy men; nor be displeased at the hard sayings of older men than thou, for they are not uttered without cause.

CHAPTER VI

Of inordinate affections

Whensoever a man desireth aught above measure, immediately he becometh restless. The proud and the avaricious man are never at rest; while the poor and lowly of heart abide in the multitude of peace. The man who is not yet wholly dead to self, is soon tempted, and is overcome in small and trifling matters. It is hard for him who is weak in spirit, and still in part carnal and inclined to the pleasures of sense, to withdraw himself altogether from earthly desires. And therefore, when he withdraweth himself from these, he is often sad, and easily angered too if any oppose his will.

2. But if, on the other hand, he yield to his inclination, immediately he is weighed down by the condemnation of his conscience; for that he hath followed his own desire, and yet in no way attained the peace which he hoped for. For true peace of heart is to be found in resisting passion, not in yielding to it. And therefore there is no peace in the heart of a man who is carnal, nor in him who is given up to the things that are without him, but only in him who is fervent towards God and living the life of the Spirit.

CHAPTER VII

Of fleeing from vain hope and pride

Vain is the life of that man who putteth his trust in men or in any created Thing. Be not ashamed to be the servant of others for the love of Jesus Christ, and to be reckoned poor in this life. Rest not upon thyself, but build thy hope in God. Do what lieth in thy power, and God will help thy good intent. Trust not in thy learning, nor in the cleverness of any that lives, but rather trust in the favour of God, who resisteth the proud and giveth grace to the humble.

2. Boast not thyself in thy riches if thou hast them, nor in thy friends if they be powerful, but in God, who giveth all things,

and in addition to all things desireth to give even Himself. Be not lifted up because of thy strength or beauty of body, for with only a slight sickness it will fail and wither away. Be not vain of thy skilfulness or ability, lest thou displease God, from whom cometh every good gift which we have.

3. Count not thyself better than others, lest perchance thou appear worse in the sight of God, who knoweth what is in man. Be not proud of thy good works, for God's judgments are of another sort than the judgments of man, and what pleaseth man is ofttimes displeasing to Him. If thou hast any good, believe that others have more, and so thou mayest preserve thy humility. It is no harm to thee if thou place thyself below all others; but it is great harm if thou place thyself above even one. Peace is ever with the humble man, but in the heart of the proud there is envy and continual wrath.

CHAPTER VIII

Of the danger of too much familiarity

Open not thine heart to every man, but deal with one who is wise and feareth God. Be seldom with the young and with strangers. Be not a flatterer of the rich; nor willingly seek the society of the great. Let thy company be the humble and the simple, the devout and the gentle, and let thy discourse be concerning things which edify. Be not familiar with any woman, but commend all good women alike unto God. Choose for thy companions God and His Angels only, and flee from the notice of men.

2. We must love all men, but not make close companions of all. It sometimes falleth out that one who is unknown to us is highly regarded through good report of him, whose actual person is nevertheless unpleasing to those who behold it. We sometimes think to please others by our intimacy, and forthwith displease them the more by the faultiness of character which they perceive in us.

CHAPTER IX

Of obedience and subjection

It is verily a great thing to live in obedience, to be under authority, and not to be at our own disposal. Far safer is it to live in subjection than in a place of authority. Many are in obedience from necessity rather than from love; these take it amiss, and repine for small cause. Nor will they gain freedom of spirit, unless with all their heart they submit themselves for the love of God. Though thou run hither and thither, thou wilt not find peace, save in humble subjection to the authority of him who is set over thee. Fancies about places and change of them have deceived many.

2. True it is that every man willingly followeth his own bent, and is the more inclined to those who agree with him. But if Christ is amongst us, then it is necessary that we sometimes yield up our own opinion for the sake of peace. Who is so wise as to have perfect knowledge of all things? Therefore trust not too much to thine own opinion, but be ready also to hear the opinions of others. Though thine own opinion be good, yet if for the love of God thou foregoest it, and followest that of another, thou shalt the more profit thereby.

3. Ofttimes I have heard that it is safer to hearken and to receive counsel than to give it. It may also come to pass that each opinion may be good; but to refuse to hearken to others when reason or occasion requireth it, is a mark of pride or wilfulness.

CHAPTER X

Of the danger of superfluity of words

Avoid as far as thou canst the tumult of men; for talk concerning worldly things, though it be innocently undertaken, is a hindrance, so quickly are we led captive and defiled by vanity. Many a time I wish that I had held my peace, and had not gone amongst men. But why do we talk and gossip so continually, seeing that we so rarely resume our silence without some hurt done to our conscience? We like talking so much because we hope by our conversations to gain some mutual comfort, and because we seek to refresh our wearied spirits by variety of thoughts. And we very willingly talk and think of those things which we love or desire, or else of those which we most dislike.

2. But alas! it is often to no purpose and in vain. For this outward consolation is no small hindrance to the inner comfort which cometh from God. Therefore must we watch and pray that time pass not idly away. If it be right and desirable for thee to speak, speak things which are to edification. Evil custom and neglect of our real profit tend much to make us heedless of watching over our lips. Nevertheless, devout conversation on spiritual things helpeth not a little to spiritual progress, most of all where those of kindred mind and spirit find their ground of fellowship in God.

CHAPTER XI

Of seeking peace of mind and of spiritual progress

We may enjoy abundance of peace if we refrain from busying ourselves with the sayings and doings of others, and things which concern not ourselves. How can he abide long time in peace who occupieth himself with other men's matters, and with things without himself, and meanwhile payeth little or rare heed to the self within? Blessed are the single-hearted, for they shall have abundance of peace.

2. How came it to pass that many of the Saints were so perfect, so contemplative of Divine things? Because they steadfastly sought to mortify themselves from all worldly desires, and so were enabled to cling with their whole heart to God, and be free and at leisure for the thought of Him. We are too much occupied with our own affections, and too anxious about transitory things. Seldom, too, do we entirely conquer even a single fault, nor are we zealous for daily growth in grace. And so we remain lukewarm and unspiritual.

3. Were we fully watchful of ourselves, and not bound in spirit to outward things, then might we be wise unto salvation, and make progress in Divine contemplation. Our great and grievous stumbling-block is that, not being freed from our affections and desires, we strive not to enter into the perfect way of the Saints. And when even a little trouble befalleth us, too quickly are we cast down, and fly to the world to give us comfort.

4. If we would quit ourselves like men, and strive to stand firm in the battle, then should we see the Lord helping us from Heaven. For He Himself is alway ready to help those who strive and who trust in Him; yea, He provideth for us occasions of striving, to the end that we may win the victory. If we look upon our progress in religion as a progress only in outward observances and forms, our devoutness will soon come to an end. But let us lay the axe to the very root of our life, that, being cleansed from affections, we may possess our souls in peace.

5. If each year should see one fault rooted out from us, we should go quickly on to perfection. But on the contrary, we often feel that we were better and holier in the beginning of our conversion than after many years of profession. Zeal and progress ought to increase day by day; yet now it seemeth a great thing if one is able to retain some portion of his first ardour. If we would put some slight stress on ourselves at the beginning, then afterwards we should be able to do all things with ease and joy.

6. It is a hard thing to break through a habit, and a yet harder thing to go contrary to our own will. Yet if thou overcome not slight and easy obstacles, how shalt thou overcome greater ones? Withstand thy will at the beginning, and unlearn an evil habit, lest it lead thee little by little into worse difficulties. Oh, if thou knewest what peace to thyself thy holy life should bring to thyself, and what joy to others, methinketh thou wouldst be more zealous for spiritual profit.

CHAPTER XII

Of the uses of adversity

It is good for us that we sometimes have sorrows and adversities, for they often make a man lay to heart that he is only a stranger and sojourner, and may not put his trust in any worldly thing. It is good that we sometimes endure contradictions, and are hardly and unfairly judged, when we do and mean what is good. For these things help us to be humble, and shield us from vain-glory. For then we seek the more earnestly the witness of God, when men speak evil of us falsely, and give us no credit for good.

2. Therefore ought a man to rest wholly upon God, so that he needeth not seek much comfort at the hand of men. When a man who feareth God is afflicted or tried or oppressed with evil thoughts, then he seeth that God is the more necessary unto him, since without God he can do no good thing. Then he is heavy of heart, he groaneth, he crieth out for the very disquietness of his heart. Then he groweth weary of life, and would fain depart and be with Christ. By all this he is taught that in the world there can be no perfect security or fulness of peace.

CHAPTER XIII

Of resisting temptation

So long as we live in the world, we cannot be without trouble and trial. Wherefore it is written in Job, The life of man upon the earth is a trial.(1) And therefore ought each of us to give heed concerning trials and temptations, and watch unto prayer, lest the devil find occasion to deceive; for he never sleepeth, but goeth about seeking whom he may devour. No man is so perfect in holiness that he hath never temptations, nor can we ever be wholly free from them.

2. Yet, notwithstanding, temptations turn greatly unto our profit, even though they be great and hard to bear; for through them we are humbled, purified, instructed. All Saints have passed through much tribulation and temptation, and have profited thereby. And they who endured not temptation became reprobate and fell away. There is no position so sacred, no place so

secret, that it is without temptations and adversities.

3. There is no man wholly free from temptations so long as he liveth, because we have the root of temptation within ourselves, in that we are born in concupiscence. One temptation or sorrow passeth, and another cometh; and always we shall have somewhat to suffer, for we have fallen from perfect happiness. Many who seek to fly from temptations fall yet more deeply into them. By flight alone we cannot overcome, but by endurance and true humility we are made stronger than all our enemies.

4. He who only resisteth outwardly and pulleth not up by the root, shall profit little; nay, rather temptations will return to him the more quickly, and will be the more terrible. Little by little, through patience and longsuffering, thou shalt conquer by the help of God, rather than by violence and thine own strength of will. In the midst of temptation often seek counsel; and deal not hardly with one who is tempted, but comfort and strengthen him as thou wouldest have done unto thyself.

5. The beginning of all temptations to evil is instability of temper and want of trust in God; for even as a ship without a helm is tossed about by the waves, so is a man who is careless and infirm of purpose tempted, now on this side, now on that. As fire testeth iron, so doth temptation the upright man. Oftentimes we know not what strength we have; but temptation revealeth to us what we are. Nevertheless, we must watch, especially in the beginnings of temptation; for then is the foe the more easily mastered, when he is not suffered to enter within the mind, but is met outside the door as soon as he hath knocked. Wherefore one saith,

   Check the beginnings; once thou might'st have cured,
   But now 'tis past thy skill, too long hath it endured.

For first cometh to the mind the simple suggestion, then the strong imagination, afterwards pleasure, evil affection, assent. And so little by little the enemy entereth in altogether, because he was not resisted at the beginning. And the longer a man delayeth his resistance, the weaker he groweth, and the stronger groweth the enemy against him.

6. Some men suffer their most grievous temptations in the beginning of their conversion, some at the end. Some are sorely tried their whole life long. Some there are who are tempted but lightly, according to the wisdom and justice of the ordering of God, who knoweth the character and circumstances of men, and ordereth all things for the welfare of His elect.

7. Therefore we ought not to despair when we are tempted, but the more fervently should cry unto God, that He will vouchsafe to help us in all our tribulation; and that He will, as St. Paul saith, with the temptation make a way to escape that we may be able to bear it.(2) Let us therefore humble ourselves under the mighty hand of God in all temptation and trouble, for He will save and exalt such as are of an humble spirit.

8. In temptations and troubles a man is proved, what progress he hath made, and therein is his reward the greater, and his virtue doth the more appear. Nor is it a great thing if a man be devout and zealous so long as he suffereth no affliction; but if he behave himself patiently in the time of adversity, then is there hope of great progress. Some are kept safe from great temptations, but are overtaken in those which are little and common, that the humiliation may teach them not to trust to themselves in great things, being weak in small things.

(1) Job vii. 1 (Vulg.).   (2) 1 Corinthians x. 13.

CHAPTER XIV

On avoiding rash judgment

Look well unto thyself, and beware that thou judge not the doings of others. In judging others a man laboureth in vain; he often erreth, and easily falleth into sin; but in judging and examining himself he always laboureth to good purpose. According as a matter toucheth our fancy, so oftentimes do we judge of it; for easily do we fail of true judgment because of our own personal feeling. If God were always the sole object of our desire, we should the less easily be troubled by the erring judgment of our fancy.

2. But often some secret thought lurking within us, or even some outward circumstance, turneth us aside. Many are secretly seeking their own ends in what they do, yet know it not. They seem to live in good peace of mind so long as things go well with them, and according to their desires, but if their desires be frustrated and broken, immediately they are shaken and displeased. Diversity of feelings and opinions very often brings about dissensions between friends, between countrymen, between religious and godly men.

3. Established custom is not easily relinquished, and no man is very easily led to see with the eyes of another. If thou rest more upon thy own reason or experience than upon the power of Jesus Christ, thy light shall come slowly and hardly; for God willeth us to be perfectly subject unto Himself, and all our reason to be exalted by abundant love towards Him.

CHAPTER XV

Of works of charity

For no worldly good whatsoever, and for the love of no man, must anything be done which is evil, but for the help of the suffering a good work must sometimes be postponed, or be changed for a better; for herein a good work is not destroyed, but improved. Without charity no work profiteth, but whatsoever is done in charity, however small and of no reputation it be, bringeth forth good fruit; for God verily considereth what a man is able to do, more than the greatness of what he doth.

2. He doth much who loveth much. He doth much who doth well. He doth well who ministereth to the public good rather than to his own. Oftentimes that seemeth to be charity which is rather carnality, because it springeth from natural inclination, self-will, hope of repayment, desire of gain.

3. He who hath true and perfect charity, in no wise seeketh his own good, but desireth that God alone be altogether glorified.

He envieth none, because he longeth for no selfish joy; nor doth he desire to rejoice in himself, but longeth to be blessed in God as the highest good. He ascribeth good to none save to God only, the Fountain whence all good proceedeth, and the End, the Peace, the joy of all Saints. Oh, he who hath but a spark of true charity, hath verily learned that all worldly things are full of vanity.

CHAPTER XVI

Of bearing with the faults of others

Those things which a man cannot amend in himself or in others, he ought patiently to bear, until God shall otherwise ordain. Bethink thee that perhaps it is better for thy trial and patience, without which our merits are but little worth. Nevertheless thou oughtest, when thou findeth such impediments, to beseech God that He would vouchsafe to sustain thee, that thou be able to bear them with a good will.

2. If one who is once or twice admonished refuse to hearken, strive not with him, but commit all to God, that His will may be done and His honour be shown in His servants, for He knoweth well how to convert the evil unto good. Endeavour to be patient in bearing with other men's faults and infirmities whatsoever they be, for thou thyself also hast many things which have need to be borne with by others. If thou canst not make thine own self what thou desireth, how shalt thou be able to fashion another to thine own liking. We are ready to see others made perfect, and yet we do not amend our own shortcomings.

3. We will that others be straitly corrected, but we will not be corrected ourselves. The freedom of others displeaseth us, but we are dissatisfied that our own wishes shall be denied us. We desire rules to be made restraining others, but by no means will we suffer ourselves to be restrained. Thus therefore doth it plainly appear how seldom we weigh our neighbour in the same balance with ourselves. If all men were perfect, what then should we have to suffer from others for God?

4. But now hath God thus ordained, that we may learn to bear one

another's burdens, because none is without defect, none without a burden, none sufficient of himself, none wise enough of himself; but it behoveth us to bear with one another, to comfort one another, to help, instruct, admonish one another. How much strength each man hath is best proved by occasions of adversity: for such occasions do not make a man frail, but show of what temper he is.

CHAPTER XVII

Of a religious life

It behoveth thee to learn to mortify thyself in many things, if thou wilt live in amity and concord with other men. It is no small thing to dwell in a religious community or congregation, and to live there without complaint, and therein to remain faithful even unto death. Blessed is he who hath lived a good life in such a body, and brought it to a happy end. If thou wilt stand fast and wilt profit as thou oughtest, hold thyself as an exile and a pilgrim upon the earth. Thou wilt have to be counted as a fool for Christ, if thou wilt lead a religious life.

2. The clothing and outward appearance are of small account; it is change of character and entire mortification of the affections which make a truly religious man. He who seeketh aught save God and the health of his soul, shall find only tribulation and sorrow. Nor can he stand long in peace, who striveth not to be least of all and servant of all.

3. Thou art called to endure and to labour, not to a life of ease and trifling talk. Here therefore are men tried as gold in the furnace. No man can stand, unless with all his heart he will humble himself for God's sake.

CHAPTER XVIII

Of the example of the Holy Fathers

Consider now the lively examples of the holy fathers, in whom shone forth real perfectness and religion, and thou shalt see how little, even as nothing, is all that we do. Ah! What is our life when compared to theirs? They, saints and friends of Christ as they were, served the Lord in hunger and thirst, in cold and nakedness, in labour and weariness, in watchings and fastings, in prayer and holy meditations, in persecutions and much rebuke.

2. O how many and grievous tribulations did the Apostles, Martyrs, Confessors, Virgins, endure; and all others who would walk in the footsteps of Christ. For they hated their souls in this world that they might keep them unto life eternal. O how strict and retired a life was that of the holy fathers who dwelt in the desert! what long and grievous temptations they did suffer! how often were they assaulted by the enemy! what frequent and fervid prayers did they offer unto God! what strict fasts did they endure! what fervent zeal and desire after spiritual profit did they manifest! how bravely did they fight that their vices might not gain the mastery! how entirely and steadfastly did they reach after God! By day they laboured, and at night they gave themselves ofttimes unto prayer; yea, even when they were labouring they ceased not from mental prayer.

3. They spent their whole time profitably; every hour seemed short for retirement with God; and through the great sweetness of contemplation, even the need of bodily refreshment was forgotten. They renounced all riches, dignities, honours, friends, kinsmen; they desired nothing from the world; they ate the bare necessaries of life; they were unwilling to minister to the body even in necessity. Thus were they poor in earthly things, but rich above measure in grace and virtue. Though poor to the outer eye, within they were filled with grace and heavenly benedictions.

4. They were strangers to the world, but unto God they were as kinsmen and friends. They seemed unto themselves as of no reputation, and in the world's eyes contemptible; but in the sight of God they were precious and beloved. They stood fast in true humility, they lived in simple obedience, they walked in love and patience; and thus they waxed strong in spirit, and obtained great favour before God. To all religious men they were given as an example, and they ought more to provoke us unto good

livings than the number of the lukewarm tempteth to carelessness of life.

5. O how great was the love of all religious persons at the beginning of this sacred institution! O what devoutness of prayer! what rivalry in holiness! what strict discipline was observed! what reverence and obedience under the rule of the master showed they in all things! The traces of them that remain until now testify that they were truly holy and perfect men, who fighting so bravely trod the world underfoot. Now a man is counted great if only he be not a transgressor, and if he can only endure with patience what he hath undertaken.

6. O the coldness and negligence of our times, that we so quickly decline from the former love, and it is become a weariness to live, because of sloth and lukewarmness. May progress in holiness not wholly fall asleep in thee, who many times hast seen so many examples of devout men!

CHAPTER XIX

Of the exercises of a religious man

The life of a Christian ought to be adorned with all virtues, that he may be inwardly what he outwardly appeareth unto men. And verily it should be yet better within than without, for God is a discerner of our heart, Whom we must reverence with all our hearts wheresoever we are, and walk pure in His presence as do the angels. We ought daily to renew our vows, and to kindle our hearts to zeal, as if each day were the first day of our conversion, and to say, "Help me, O God, in my good resolutions, and in Thy holy service, and grant that this day I may make a good beginning, for hitherto I have done nothing!"

2. According to our resolution so is the rate of our progress, and much diligence is needful for him who would make good progress. For if he who resolveth bravely oftentimes falleth short, how shall it be with him who resolveth rarely or feebly? But manifold causes bring about abandonment of our resolution, yet a trivial omission of holy exercises can hardly be made

without some loss to us. The resolution of the righteous dependeth more upon the grace of God than upon their own wisdom; for in Him they always put their trust, whatsoever they take in hand. For man proposeth, but God disposeth; and the way of a man is not in himself.(1)

3. If a holy exercise be sometimes omitted for the sake of some act of piety, or of some brotherly kindness, it can easily be taken up afterwards; but if it be neglected through distaste or slothfulness, then is it sinful, and the mischief will be felt. Strive as earnestly as we may, we shall still fall short in many things. Always should some distinct resolution be made by us; and, most of all, we must strive against those sins which most easily beset us. Both our outer and inner life should be straitly examined and ruled by us, because both have to do with our progress.

4. If thou canst not be always examining thyself, thou canst at certain seasons, and at least twice in the day, at evening and at morning. In the morning make thy resolves, and in the evening inquire into thy life, how thou hast sped to-day in word, deed, and thought; for in these ways thou hast often perchance offended God and thy neighbour. Gird up thy lions like a man against the assaults of the devil; bridle thine appetite, and thou wilt soon be able to bridle every inclination of the flesh. Be thou never without something to do; be reading, or writing, or praying, or meditating, or doing something that is useful to the community. Bodily exercises, however, must be undertaken with discretion, nor are they to be used by all alike.

5. The duties which are not common to all must not be done openly, but are safest carried on in secret. But take heed that thou be not careless in the common duties, and more devout in the secret; but faithfully and honestly discharge the duties and commands which lie upon thee, then afterwards, if thou hast still leisure, give thyself to thyself as thy devotion leadeth thee. All cannot have one exercise, but one suiteth better to this man and another to that. Even for the diversity of season different exercises are needed, some suit better for feasts, some for fasts. We need one kind in time of temptations and others in time of peace and quietness. Some are suitable to our times of

sadness, and others when we are joyful in the Lord.

6. When we draw near the time of the great feasts, good exercises should be renewed, and the prayers of holy men more fervently besought. We ought to make our resolutions from one Feast to another, as if each were the period of our departure from this world, and of entering into the eternal feast. So ought we to prepare ourselves earnestly at solemn seasons, and the more solemnly to live, and to keep straightest watch upon each holy observance, as though we were soon to receive the reward of our labours at the hand of God.

7. And if this be deferred, let us believe ourselves to be as yet ill-prepared, and unworthy as yet of the glory which shall be revealed in us at the appointed season; and let us study to prepare ourselves the better for our end. Blessed is that servant, as the Evangelist Luke hath it, whom, when the Lord cometh He shall find watching. Verily I say unto you He will make him ruler over all that He hath.(2)

(1) Jeremiah x. 23.   (2) Luke xii. 43, 44.

CHAPTER XX

Of the love of solitude and silence

Seek a suitable time for thy meditation, and think frequently of the mercies of God to thee. Leave curious questions. Study such matters as bring thee sorrow for sin rather than amusement. If thou withdraw thyself from trifling conversation and idle goings about, as well as from novelties and gossip, thou shalt find thy time sufficient and apt for good meditation. The greatest saints used to avoid as far as they could the company of men, and chose to live in secret with God.

2. One hath said, "As oft as I have gone among men, so oft have I returned less a man." This is what we often experience when we have been long time in conversation. For it is easier to be altogether silent than it is not to exceed in word. It is easier to remain hidden at home than to keep sufficient guard upon

thyself out of doors. He, therefore, that seeketh to reach that which is hidden and spiritual, must go with Jesus "apart from the multitude." No man safely goeth abroad who loveth not to rest at home. No man safely talketh but he who loveth to hold his peace. No man safely ruleth but he who loveth to be subject. No man safely commandeth but he who loveth to obey.

3. No man safely rejoiceth but he who hath the testimony of a good conscience within himself. The boldness of the Saints was always full of the fear of God. Nor were they the less earnest and humble in themselves, because they shone forth with great virtues and grace. But the boldness of wicked men springeth from pride and presumption, and at the last turneth to their own confusion. Never promise thyself security in this life, howsoever good a monk or devout a solitary thou seemest.

4. Often those who stand highest in the esteem of men, fall the more grievously because of their over great confidence. Wherefore it is very profitable unto many that they should not be without inward temptation, but should be frequently assaulted, lest they be over confident, lest they be indeed lifted up into pride, or else lean too freely upon the consolations of the world. O how good a conscience should that man keep, who never sought a joy that passeth away, who never became entangled with the world! O how great peace and quiet should he possess, who would cast off all vain care, and think only of healthful and divine things, and build his whole hope upon God!

5. No man is worthy of heavenly consolation but he who hath diligently exercised himself in holy compunction. If thou wilt feel compunction within thy heart, enter into thy chamber and shut out the tumults of the world, as it is written, Commune with your own heart in your own chamber and be still.(1) In retirement thou shalt find what often thou wilt lose abroad. Retirement, if thou continue therein, groweth sweet, but if thou keep not in it, begetteth weariness. If in the beginning of thy conversation thou dwell in it and keep it well, it shall afterwards be to thee a dear friend, and a most pleasant solace.

6. In silence and quiet the devout soul goeth forward and learneth the hidden things of the Scriptures. Therein findeth

she a fountain of tears, wherein to wash and cleanse herself each night, that she may grow the more dear to her Maker as she dwelleth the further from all worldly distraction. To him who withdraweth himself from his acquaintance and friends God with his holy angels will draw nigh. It is better to be unknown and take heed to oneself than to neglect oneself and work wonders. It is praiseworthy for a religious man to go seldom abroad, to fly from being seen, to have no desire to see men.

7. Why wouldest thou see what thou mayest not have? The world passeth away and the lust thereof. The desires of sensuality draw thee abroad, but when an hour is past, what dost thou bring home, but a weight upon thy conscience and distraction of heart? A merry going forth bringeth often a sorrowful return, and a merry evening maketh a sad morning? So doth all carnal joy begin pleasantly, but in the end it gnaweth away and destroyeth. What canst thou see abroad which thou seest not at home? Behold the heaven and the earth and the elements, for out of these are all things made.

8. What canst thou see anywhere which can continue long under the sun? Thou believest perchance that thou shalt be satisfied, but thou wilt never be able to attain unto this. If thou shouldest see all things before thee at once, what would it be but a vain vision? Lift up thine eyes to God on high, and pray that thy sins and negligences may be forgiven. Leave vain things to vain men, and mind thou the things which God hath commanded thee. Shut thy door upon thee, and call unto thyself Jesus thy beloved. Remain with Him in thy chamber, for thou shalt not elsewhere find so great peace. If thou hadst not gone forth nor listened to vain talk, thou hadst better kept thyself in good peace. But because it sometimes delighteth thee to hear new things, thou must therefore suffer trouble of heart.

(1) Psalm iv. 4.

CHAPTER XXI

Of compunction of heart

If thou wilt make any progress keep thyself in the fear of God, and long not to be too free, but restrain all thy senses under discipline and give not thyself up to senseless mirth. Give thyself to compunction of heart and thou shalt find devotion. Compunction openeth the way for many good things, which dissoluteness is wont quickly to lose. It is wonderful that any man can ever rejoice heartily in this life who considereth and weigheth his banishment, and the manifold dangers which beset his soul.

2. Through lightness of heart and neglect of our shortcomings we feel not the sorrows of our soul, but often vainly laugh when we have good cause to weep. There is no true liberty nor real joy, save in the fear of God with a good conscience. Happy is he who can cast away every cause of distraction and bring himself to the one purpose of holy compunction. Happy is he who putteth away from him whatsoever may stain or burden his conscience. Strive manfully; custom is overcome by custom. If thou knowest how to let men alone, they will gladly let thee alone to do thine own works.

3. Busy not thyself with the affairs of others, nor entangle thyself with the business of great men. Keep always thine eye upon thyself first of all, and give advice to thyself specially before all thy dearest friends. If thou hast not the favour of men, be not thereby cast down, but let thy concern be that thou holdest not thyself so well and circumspectly, as becometh a servant of God and a devout monk. It is often better and safer for a man not to have many comforts in this life, especially those which concern the flesh. But that we lack divine comforts or feel them rarely is to our own blame, because we seek not compunction of heart, nor utterly cast away those comforts which are vain and worldly.

4. Know thyself to be unworthy of divine consolation, and worthy rather of much tribulation. When a man hath perfect compunction,

then all the world is burdensome and bitter to him. A good man will find sufficient cause for mourning and weeping; for whether he considereth himself, or pondereth concerning his neighbour, he knoweth that no man liveth here without tribulation, and the more thoroughly he considereth himself, the more thoroughly he grieveth. Grounds for just grief and inward compunction there are in our sins and vices, wherein we lie so entangled that we are but seldom able to contemplate heavenly things.

5. If thou thoughtest upon thy death more often than how long thy life should be, thou wouldest doubtless strive more earnestly to improve. And if thou didst seriously consider the future pains of hell, I believe thou wouldest willingly endure toil or pain and fear not discipline. But because these things reach not the heart, and we still love pleasant things, therefore we remain cold and miserably indifferent.

6. Oftentimes it is from poverty of spirit that the wretched body is so easily led to complain. Pray therefore humbly unto the Lord that He will give thee the spirit of compunction and say in the language of the prophet, Feed me, O Lord, with bread of tears, and give me plenteousness of tears to drink.(1)

(1) Psalm lxxv. 5.

CHAPTER XXII

On the contemplation of human misery

Thou art miserable wheresoever thou art, and whithersoever thou turnest, unless thou turn thee to God. Why art thou disquieted because it happeneth not to thee according to thy wishes and desires? Who is he that hath everything according to his will? Neither I, nor thou, nor any man upon the earth. There is no man in the world free from trouble or anguish, though he were King or Pope. Who is he who hath the happiest lot? Even he who is strong to suffer somewhat for God.

2. There are many foolish and unstable men who say, "See what a prosperous life that man hath, how rich and how great he is, how

powerful, how exalted." But lift up thine eyes to the good things of heaven, and thou shalt see that all these worldly things are nothing, they are utterly uncertain, yea, they are wearisome, because they are never possessed without care and fear. The happiness of man lieth not in the abundance of temporal things but a moderate portion sufficeth him. Our life upon the earth is verily wretchedness. The more a man desireth to be spiritual, the more bitter doth the present life become to him; because he the better understandeth and seeth the defects of human corruption. For to eat, to drink, to watch, to sleep, to rest, to labour, and to be subject to the other necessities of nature, is truly a great wretchedness and affliction to a devout man, who would fain be released and free from all sin.

3. For the inner man is heavily burdened with the necessities of the body in this world. Wherefore the prophet devoutly prayeth to be freed from them, saying, Deliver me from my necessities, O Lord.(1) But woe to those who know not their own misery, and yet greater woe to those who love this miserable and corruptible life. For to such a degree do some cling to it (even though by labouring or begging they scarce procure what is necessary for subsistence) that if they might live here always, they would care nothing for the Kingdom of God.

4. Oh foolish and faithless of heart, who lie buried so deep in worldly things, that they relish nothing save the things of the flesh! Miserable ones! they will too sadly find out at the last, how vile and worthless was that which they loved. The saints of God and all loyal friends of Christ held as nothing the things which pleased the flesh, or those which flourished in this life, but their whole hope and affection aspired to the things which are above. Their whole desire was borne upwards to everlasting and invisible things, lest they should be drawn downwards by the love of things visible.

5. Lose not, brother, thy loyal desire of progress to things spiritual. There is yet time, the hour is not past. Why wilt thou put off thy resolution? Arise, begin this very moment, and say, "Now is the time to do: now is the time to fight, now is the proper time for amendment." When thou art ill at ease and troubled, then is the time when thou art nearest unto blessing.

Thou must go through fire and water that God may bring thee into a wealthy place. Unless thou put force upon thyself, thou wilt not conquer thy faults. So long as we carry about with us this frail body, we cannot be without sin, we cannot live without weariness and trouble. Gladly would we have rest from all misery; but because through sin we have lost innocence, we have lost also the true happiness. Therefore must we be patient, and wait for the mercy of God, until this tyranny be overpast, and this mortality be swallowed up of life.

6. O how great is the frailty of man, which is ever prone to evil! To-day thou confessest thy sins, and to-morrow thou committest again the sins thou didst confess. Now dost thou resolve to avoid a fault, and within an hour thou behavest thyself as if thou hadst never resolved at all. Good cause have we therefore to humble ourselves, and never to think highly of ourselves, seeing that we are so frail and unstable. And quickly may that be lost by our negligence, which by much labour was hardly attained through grace.

7. What shall become of us at the end, if at the beginning we are lukewarm and idle? Woe unto us, if we choose to rest, as though it were a time of peace and security, while as yet no sign appeareth in our life of true holiness. Rather had we need that we might begin yet afresh, like good novices, to be instructed unto good living, if haply there might be hope of some future amendment and greater spiritual increase.

(1) Psalm xxv. 17.

CHAPTER XXIII

Of meditation upon death

Very quickly will there be an end of thee here; take heed therefore how it will be with thee in another world. To-day man is, and to-morrow he will be seen no more. And being removed out of sight, quickly also he is out of mind. O the dulness and hardness of man's heart, which thinketh only of the present, and looketh not forward to the future. Thou oughtest in every deed and thought so to order thyself, as if thou wert to die this day. If thou hadst a good conscience thou wouldst not greatly fear death. It were better for thee to watch against sin, than to fly from death. If to-day thou art not ready, how shalt thou be ready to-morrow? To-morrow is an uncertain day; and how knowest thou that thou shalt have a to-morrow?

2. What doth it profit to live long, when we amend so little? Ah! long life doth not always amend, but often the more increaseth guilt. Oh that we might spend a single day in this world as it ought to be spent! Many there are who reckon the years since they were converted, and yet oftentimes how little is the fruit thereof. If it is a fearful thing to die, it may be perchance a yet more fearful thing to live long. Happy is the man who hath the hour of his death always before his eyes, and daily prepareth himself to die. If thou hast ever seen one die, consider that thou also shalt pass away by the same road.

3. When it is morning reflect that it may be thou shalt not see the evening, and at eventide dare not to boast thyself of the morrow. Always be thou prepared, and so live that death may never find thee unprepared. Many die suddenly and unexpectedly. For at such an hour as ye think not, the Son of Man cometh.(1) When that last hour shall come, thou wilt begin to think very differently of thy whole life past, and wilt mourn bitterly that thou hast been so negligent and slothful.

4. Happy and wise is he who now striveth to be such in life as he would fain be found in death! For a perfect contempt of the world, a fervent desire to excel in virtue, the love of discipline, the painfulness of repentance, readiness to obey, denial of self, submission to any adversity for love of Christ; these are the things which shall give great confidence of a happy death. Whilst thou art in health thou hast many opportunities of good works; but when thou art in sickness I know not how much thou wilt be able to do. Few are made better by infirmity: even as they who wander much abroad seldom become holy.

5. Trust not thy friends and kinsfolk, nor put off the work of thy salvation to the future, for men will forget thee sooner than thou thinkest. It is better for thee now to provide in time, and

to send some good before thee, than to trust to the help of others. If thou art not anxious for thyself now, who, thinkest thou, will be anxious for thee afterwards? Now the time is most precious. Now is the accepted time, now is the day of salvation. But alas! that thou spendest not well this time, wherein thou mightest lay up treasure which should profit thee everlastingly. The hour will come when thou shalt desire one day, yea, one hour, for amendment of life, and I know not whether thou shalt obtain.

6. Oh, dearly beloved, from what danger thou mightest free thyself, from what great fear, if only thou wouldst always live in fear, and in expectation of death! Strive now to live in such wise that in the hour of death thou mayest rather rejoice than fear. Learn now to die to the world, so shalt thou begin to live with Christ. Learn now to contemn all earthly things, and then mayest thou freely go unto Christ. Keep under thy body by penitence, and then shalt thou be able to have a sure confidence.

7. Ah, foolish one! why thinkest thou that thou shalt live long, when thou art not sure of a single day? How many have been deceived, and suddenly have been snatched away from the body! How many times hast thou heard how one was slain by the sword, another was drowned, another falling from on high broke his neck, another died at the table, another whilst at play! One died by fire, another by the sword, another by the pestilence, another by the robber. Thus cometh death to all, and the life of men swiftly passeth away like a shadow.

8. Who will remember thee after thy death? And who will entreat for thee? Work, work now, oh dearly beloved, work all that thou canst. For thou knowest not when thou shalt die, nor what shall happen unto thee after death. While thou hast time, lay up for thyself undying riches. Think of nought but of thy salvation; care only for the things of God. Make to thyself friends, by venerating the saints of God and walking in their steps, that when thou failest, thou mayest be received into everlasting habitations.(2)

9. Keep thyself as a stranger and a pilgrim upon the earth, to whom the things of the world appertain not. Keep thine heart free, and lifted up towards God, for here have we no continuing

city.(3) To Him direct thy daily prayers with crying and tears, that thy spirit may be found worthy to pass happily after death unto its Lord. Amen.

(1) Matthew xxiv. 44.   (2) Luke xvi. 9.   (3) Hebrews xiii. 14.

CHAPTER XXIV

Of the judgment and punishment of the wicked

In all that thou doest, remember the end, and how thou wilt stand before a strict judge, from whom nothing is hid, who is not bribed with gifts, nor accepteth excuses, but will judge righteous judgment. O most miserable and foolish sinner, who art sometimes in fear of the countenance of an angry man, what wilt thou answer to God, who knoweth all thy misdeeds? Why dost thou not provide for thyself against the day of judgment, when no man shall be able to be excused or defended by means of another, but each one shall bear his burden himself alone? Now doth thy labour bring forth fruit, now is thy weeping acceptable, thy groaning heard, thy sorrow well pleasing to God, and cleansing to thy soul.

2. Even here on earth the patient man findeth great occasion of purifying his soul. When suffering injuries he grieveth more for the other's malice than for his own wrong; when he prayeth heartily for those that despitefully use him, and forgiveth them from his heart; when he is not slow to ask pardon from others; when he is swifter to pity than to anger; when he frequently denieth himself and striveth altogether to subdue the flesh to the spirit. Better is it now to purify the soul from sin, than to cling to sins from which we must be purged hereafter. Truly we deceive ourselves by the inordinate love which we bear towards the flesh.

3. What is it which that fire shall devour, save thy sins? The more thou sparest thyself and followest the flesh, the more heavy shall thy punishment be, and the more fuel art thou heaping up for the burning. For wherein a man hath sinned, therein shall he be the more heavily punished. There shall the slothful be

pricked forward with burning goads, and the gluttons be tormented with intolerable hunger and thirst. There shall the luxurious and the lovers of pleasure be plunged into burning pitch and stinking brimstone, and the envious shall howl like mad dogs for very grief.

4. No sin will there be which shall not be visited with its own proper punishment. The proud shall be filled with utter confusion, and the covetous shall be pinched with miserable poverty. An hour's pain there shall be more grievous than a hundred years here of the bitterest penitence. No quiet shall be there, no comfort for the lost, though here sometimes there is respite from pain, and enjoyment of the solace of friends. Be thou anxious now and sorrowful for thy sins, that in the day of judgment thou mayest have boldness with the blessed. For then shall the righteous man stand in great boldness before the face of such as have afflicted him and made no account of his labours.(1) Then shall he stand up to judge, he who now submitteth himself in humility to the judgments of men. Then shall the poor and humble man have great confidence, while the proud is taken with fear on every side.

5. Then shall it be seen that he was the wise man in this world who learned to be a fool and despised for Christ. Then shall all tribulation patiently borne delight us, while the mouth of the ungodly shall be stopped. Then shall every godly man rejoice, and every profane man shall mourn. Then the afflicted flesh shall more rejoice than if it had been alway nourished in delights. Then the humble garment shall put on beauty, and the precious robe shall hide itself as vile. Then the little poor cottage shall be more commended than the gilded palace. Then enduring patience shall have more might than all the power of the world. Then simple obedience shall be more highly exalted than all worldly wisdom.

6. Then a pure and good conscience shall more rejoice than learned philosophy. Then contempt of riches shall have more weight than all the treasure of the children of this world. Then shalt thou find more comfort in having prayed devoutly than in having fared sumptuously. Then thou wilt rather rejoice in having kept silence than in having made long speech. Then holy

deeds shall be far stronger than many fine words. Then a strict life and sincere penitence shall bring deeper pleasure than all earthly delight. Learn now to suffer a little, that then thou mayest be enabled to escape heavier sufferings. Prove first here, what thou art able to endure hereafter. If now thou art able to bear so little, how wilt thou be able to endure eternal torments? If now a little suffering maketh thee so impatient, what shall hell-fire do then? Behold of a surety thou art not able to have two Paradises, to take thy fill or delight here in this world, and to reign with Christ hereafter.

7. If even unto this day thou hadst ever lived in honours and pleasures, what would the whole profit thee if now death came to thee in an instant? All therefore is vanity, save to love God and to serve Him only. For he who loveth God with all his heart feareth not death, nor punishment, nor judgment, nor hell, because perfect love giveth sure access to God. But he who still delighteth in sin, no marvel if he is afraid of death and judgment. Nevertheless it is a good thing, if love as yet cannot restrain thee from evil, that at least the fear of hell should hold thee back. But he who putteth aside the fear of God cannot long continue in good, but shall quickly fall into the snares of the devil.

(1) Wisd. v. 1.

CHAPTER XXV

Of the zealous amendment of our whole life

Be thou watchful and diligent in God's service, and bethink thee often why thou hast renounced the world. Was it not that thou mightest live to God and become a spiritual man? Be zealous, therefore, for thy spiritual profit, for thou shalt receive shortly the reward of thy labours, and neither fear nor sorrow shall come any more into thy borders. Now shalt thou labour a little, and thou shalt find great rest, yea everlasting joy. If thou shalt remain faithful and zealous in labour, doubt not that God shall be faithful and bountiful in rewarding thee. It is thy duty to have a good hope that thou wilt attain the victory, but thou must not fall into security lest thou become slothful or lifted up.

2. A certain man being in anxiety of mind, continually tossed about between hope and fear, and being on a certain day overwhelmed with grief, cast himself down in prayer before the altar in a church, and meditated within himself, saying, "Oh! if I but knew that I should still persevere," and presently heard within him a voice from God, "And if thou didst know it, what wouldst thou do? Do now what thou wouldst do then, and thou shalt be very secure." And straightway being comforted and strengthened, he committed himself to the will of God and the perturbation of spirit ceased, neither had he a mind any more to search curiously to know what should befall him hereafter, but studied rather to inquire what was the good and acceptable will of God, for the beginning and perfecting of every good work.

3. Hope in the Lord and be doing good, saith the Prophet; dwell in the land and thou shalt be fed(1) with its riches. One thing there is which holdeth back many from progress and fervent amendment, even the dread of difficulty, or the labour of the conflict. Nevertheless they advance above all others in virtue who strive manfully to conquer those things which are most grievous and contrary to them, for there a man profiteth most and meriteth greater grace where he most overcometh himself and mortifieth himself in spirit.

4. But all men have not the same passions to conquer and to mortify, yet he who is diligent shall attain more profit, although he have stronger passions, than another who is more temperate of disposition, but is withal less fervent in the pursuit of virtue. Two things specially avail unto improvement in holiness, namely firmness to withdraw ourselves from the sin to which by nature we are most inclined, and earnest zeal for that good in which we are most lacking. And strive also very earnestly to guard against and subdue those faults which displease thee most frequently in others.

5. Gather some profit to thy soul wherever thou art, and wherever thou seest or hearest good examples, stir thyself to follow them, but where thou seest anything which is blameworthy, take heed

that thou do not the same; or if at any time thou hast done it, strive quickly to amend thyself. As thine eye observeth others, so again are the eyes of others upon thee. How sweet and pleasant is it to see zealous and godly brethren temperate and of good discipline; and how sad is it and grievous to see them walking disorderly, not practising the duties to which they are called. How hurtful a thing it is to neglect the purpose of their calling, and turn their inclinations to things which are none of their business.

6. Be mindful of the duties which thou hast undertaken, and set always before thee the remembrance of the Crucified. Truly oughtest thou to be ashamed as thou lookest upon the life of Jesus Christ, because thou hast not yet endeavoured to conform thyself more unto Him, though thou hast been a long time in the way of God. A religious man who exercises himself seriously and devoutly in the most holy life and passion of our Lord shall find there abundantly all things that are profitable and necessary for him, neither is there need that he shall seek anything better beyond Jesus. Oh! if Jesus crucified would come into our hearts, how quickly, and completely should we have learned all that we need to know!

7. He who is earnest receiveth and beareth well all things that are laid upon him. He who is careless and lukewarm hath trouble upon trouble, and suffereth anguish upon every side, because he is without inward consolation, and is forbidden to seek that which is outward. He who is living without discipline is exposed to grievous ruin. He who seeketh easier and lighter discipline shall always be in distress, because one thing or another will give him displeasure.

8. O! if no other duty lay upon us but to praise the Lord our God with our whole heart and voice! Oh! if thou never hadst need to eat or drink, or sleep, but wert always able to praise God, and to give thyself to spiritual exercises alone; then shouldst thou be far happier than now, when for so many necessities thou must serve the flesh. O! that these necessities were not, but only the spiritual refreshments of the soul, which alas we taste too seldom.

9. When a man hath come to this, that he seeketh comfort from no created thing, then doth he perfectly begin to enjoy God, then also will he be well contented with whatsoever shall happen unto him. Then will he neither rejoice for much nor be sorrowful for little, but he committeth himself altogether and with full trust unto God, who is all in all to him, to whom nothing perisheth nor dieth, but all things live to Him and obey His every word without delay.

10. Remember always thine end, and how the time which is lost returneth not. Without care and diligence thou shalt never get virtue. If thou beginnest to grow cold, it shall begin to go ill with thee, but if thou givest thyself unto zeal thou shalt find much peace, and shalt find thy labour the lighter because of the grace of God and the love of virtue. A zealous and diligent man is ready for all things. It is greater labour to resist sins and passions than to toil in bodily labours. He who shunneth not small faults falleth little by little into greater. At eventide thou shalt always be glad if thou spend the day profitably. Watch over thyself, stir thyself up, admonish thyself, and howsoever it be with others, neglect not thyself. The more violence thou dost unto thyself, the more thou shall profit. Amen.

(1) Psalm xxxvii. 3.

THE SECOND BOOK

ADMONITIONS CONCERNING THE INNER LIFE

CHAPTER I

Of the inward life

The kingdom of God is within you,(1) saith the Lord. Turn thee with all thine heart to the Lord and forsake this miserable world, and thou shalt find rest unto thy soul. Learn to despise outward things and to give thyself to things inward, and thou shalt see the kingdom of God come within thee. For the kingdom of God is peace and joy in the Holy Ghost, and it is not given to the wicked. Christ will come to thee, and show thee His consolation, if thou prepare a worthy mansion for Him within thee. All His glory and beauty is from within, and there it pleaseth Him to dwell. He often visiteth the inward man and holdeth with him sweet discourse, giving him soothing consolation, much peace, friendship exceeding wonderful.

2. Go to, faithful soul, prepare thy heart for this bridegroom that he may vouchsafe to come to thee and dwell within thee, for so He saith, if any man loveth me he will keep my words: and my Father will love him, and we will come unto him and make our abode with him.(2) Give, therefore, place to Christ and refuse entrance to all others. When thou hast Christ, thou art rich, and hast sufficient. He shall be thy provider and faithful watchman in all things, so that thou hast no need to trust in men, for men soon change and swiftly pass away, but Christ remaineth for ever and standeth by us firmly even to the end.

3. There is no great trust to be placed in a frail and mortal man, even though he be useful and dear to us, neither should much sorrow arise within us if sometimes he oppose and contradict us. They who are on thy side to-day, may to-morrow be against thee, and often are they turned round like the wind. Put thy whole trust in God and let Him be thy fear and thy love, He will

answer for thee Himself, and will do for thee what is best. Here hast thou no continuing city,(3) and wheresoever thou art, thou art a stranger and a pilgrim, and thou shalt never have rest unless thou art closely united to Christ within thee.

4. Why dost thou cast thine eyes hither and thither, since this is not the place of thy rest? In heaven ought thy habitation to be, and all earthly things should be looked upon as it were in the passing by. All things pass away and thou equally with them. Look that thou cleave not to them lest thou be taken with them and perish. Let thy contemplation be on the Most High, and let thy supplication be directed unto Christ without ceasing. If thou canst not behold high and heavenly things, rest thou in the passion of Christ and dwell willingly in His sacred wounds. For if thou devoutly fly to the wounds of Jesus, and the precious marks of the nails and the spear, thou shalt find great comfort in tribulation, nor will the slights of men trouble thee much, and thou wilt easily bear their unkind words.

5. Christ also, when He was in the world, was despised and rejected of men, and in His greatest necessity was left by His acquaintance and friends to bear these reproaches. Christ was willing to suffer and be despised, and darest thou complain of any? Christ had adversaries and gainsayers, and dost thou wish to have all men thy friends and benefactors? Whence shall thy patience attain her crown if no adversity befall thee? If thou art unwilling to suffer any adversity, how shalt thou be the friend of Christ? Sustain thyself with Christ and for Christ if thou wilt reign with Christ.

6. If thou hadst once entered into the mind of Jesus, and hadst tasted yea even a little of his tender love, then wouldst thou care nought for thine own convenience or inconvenience, but wouldst rather rejoice at trouble brought upon thee, because the love of Jesus maketh a man to despise himself. He who loveth Jesus, and is inwardly true and free from inordinate affections, is able to turn himself readily unto God, and to rise above himself in spirit, and to enjoy fruitful peace.

7. He who knoweth things as they are and not as they are said or seem to be, he truly is wise, and is taught of God more than of

men. He who knoweth how to walk from within, and to set little value upon outward things, requireth not places nor waiteth for seasons, for holding his intercourse with God. The inward man quickly recollecteth himself, because he is never entirely given up to outward things. No outward labour and no necessary occupations stand in his way, but as events fall out, so doth he fit himself to them. He who is rightly disposed and ordered within careth not for the strange and perverse conduct of men. A man is hindered and distracted in so far as he is moved by outward things.

8. If it were well with thee, and thou wert purified from evil, all things would work together for thy good and profiting. For this cause do many things displease thee and often trouble thee, that thou art not yet perfectly dead to thyself nor separated from all earthly things. Nothing so defileth and entangleth the heart of man as impure love towards created things. If thou rejectest outward comfort thou wilt be able to contemplate heavenly things and frequently to be joyful inwardly.

(1) Luke xvii. 21. (2) John xiv. 23. (3) Hebrews xiii. 14.

CHAPTER II

Of lowly submission

Make no great account who is for thee or against thee, but mind only the present duty and take care that God be with thee in whatsoever thou doest. Have a good conscience and God will defend thee, for he whom God will help no man's perverseness shall be able to hurt. If thou knowest how to hold thy peace and to suffer, without doubt thou shalt see the help of the Lord. He knoweth the time and the way to deliver thee, therefore must thou resign thyself to Him. To God it belongeth to help and to deliver from all confusion. Oftentimes it is very profitable for keeping us in greater humility, that others know and rebuke our faults.

2. When a man humbleth himself for his defects, he then easily pacifieth others and quickly satisfieth those that are angered

against him. God protecteth and delivereth the humble man, He loveth and comforteth the humble man, to the humble man He inclineth Himself, on the humble He bestoweth great grace, and when he is cast down He raiseth him to glory: to the humble He revealeth His secrets, and sweetly draweth and inviteth him to Himself. The humble man having received reproach, is yet in sufficient peace, because he resteth on God and not on the world. Reckon not thyself to have profited in anywise unless thou feel thyself to be inferior to all.

CHAPTER III

Of the good, peaceable man

First keep thyself in peace, and then shalt thou be able to be a peacemaker towards others. A peaceable man doth more good than a well-learned. A passionate man turneth even good into evil and easily believeth evil; a good, peaceable man converteth all things into good. He who dwelleth in peace is suspicious of none, but he who is discontented and restless is tossed with many suspicions, and is neither quiet himself nor suffereth others to be quiet. He often saith what he ought not to say, and omitteth what it were more expedient for him to do. He considereth to what duties others are bound, and neglecteth those to which he is bound himself. Therefore be zealous first over thyself, and then mayest thou righteously be zealous concerning thy neighbour.

2. Thou knowest well how to excuse and to colour thine own deeds, but thou wilt not accept the excuses of others. It would be more just to accuse thyself and excuse thy brother. If thou wilt that others bear with thee, bear thou with others. Behold how far thou art as yet from the true charity and humility which knows not how to be angry or indignant against any save self alone. It is no great thing to mingle with the good and the meek, for this is naturally pleasing to all, and every one of us willingly enjoyeth peace and liketh best those who think with us: but to be able to live peaceably with the hard and perverse, or with the disorderly, or those who oppose us, this is a great grace and a thing much to be commended and most worthy of a man.

3. There are who keep themselves in peace and keep peace also with others, and there are who neither have peace nor suffer others to have peace; they are troublesome to others, but always more troublesome to themselves. And there are who hold themselves in peace, and study to bring others unto peace; nevertheless, all our peace in this sad life lieth in humble suffering rather than in not feeling adversities. He who best knoweth how to suffer shall possess the most peace; that man is conqueror of himself and lord of the world, the friend of Christ, and the inheritor of heaven.

CHAPTER IV

Of a pure mind and simple intention

By two wings is man lifted above earthly things, even by simplicity and purity. Simplicity ought to be in the intention, purity in the affection. Simplicity reacheth towards God, purity apprehendeth Him and tasteth Him. No good action will be distasteful to thee if thou be free within from inordinate affection. If thou reachest after and seekest, nothing but the will of God and the benefit of thy neighbour, thou wilt entirely enjoy inward liberty. If thine heart were right, then should every creature be a mirror of life and a book of holy doctrine. There is no creature so small and vile but that it showeth us the goodness of God.

2. If thou wert good and pure within, then wouldst thou look upon all things without hurt and understand them aright. A pure heart seeth the very depths of heaven and hell. Such as each one is inwardly, so judgeth he outwardly. If there is any joy in the world surely the man of pure heart possesseth it, and if there is anywhere tribulation and anguish, the evil conscience knoweth it best. As iron cast into the fire loseth rust and is made altogether glowing, so the man who turneth himself altogether unto God is freed from slothfulness and changed into a new man.

3. When a man beginneth to grow lukewarm, then he feareth a little labour, and willingly accepteth outward consolation; but when he beginneth perfectly to conquer himself and to walk manfully in the way of God, then he counteth as nothing those

things which aforetime seemed to be so grievous unto him.

CHAPTER V

Of self-esteem

We cannot place too little confidence in ourselves, because grace and understanding are often lacking to us. Little light is there within us, and what we have we quickly lose by negligence. Oftentimes we perceive not how great is our inward blindness. We often do ill and excuse it worse. Sometimes we are moved by passion and count it zeal; we blame little faults in others and pass over great faults in ourselves. Quickly enough we feel and reckon up what we bear at the hands of others, but we reflect not how much others are bearing from us. He who would weigh well and rightly his own doings would not be the man to judge severely of another.

2. The spiritually-minded man putteth care of himself before all cares; and he who diligently attendeth to himself easily keepeth silence concerning others. Thou wilt never be spiritually minded and godly unless thou art silent concerning other men's matters and take full heed to thyself. If thou think wholly upon thyself and upon God, what thou seest out of doors shall move thee little. Where art thou when thou art not present to thyself? and when thou hast overrun all things, what hath it profited thee, thyself being neglected? If thou wouldst have peace and true unity, thou must put aside all other things, and gaze only upon thyself.

3. Then thou shalt make great progress if thou keep thyself free from all temporal care. Thou shalt lamentably fall away if thou set a value upon any worldly thing. Let nothing be great, nothing high, nothing pleasing, nothing acceptable unto thee, save God Himself or the things of God. Reckon as altogether vain whatsoever consolation comes to thee from a creature. The soul that loveth God looketh not to anything that is beneath God. God alone is eternal and incomprehensible, filling all things, the solace of the soul, and the true joy of the heart.

CHAPTER VI

Of the joy of a good conscience

The testimony of a good conscience is the glory of a good man. Have a good conscience and thou shalt ever have joy. A good conscience is able to bear exceeding much, and is exceeding joyful in the midst of adversities; an evil conscience is ever fearful and unquiet. Thou shalt rest sweetly if thy heart condemn thee not. Never rejoice unless when thou hast done well. The wicked have never true joy, nor feel internal peace, for there is no peace, saith my God, to the wicked.(1) And if they say "we are in peace, there shall no harm happen unto us, and who shall dare to do us hurt?" believe them not, for suddenly shall the wrath of God rise up against them, and their deeds shall be brought to nought, and their thoughts shall perish.

2. To glory in tribulation is not grievous to him who loveth; for such glorying is glorying in the Cross of Christ. Brief is the glory which is given and received of men. Sadness always goeth hand in hand with the glory of the world. The glory of the good is in their conscience, and not in the report of men. The joy of the upright is from God and in God, and their joy is in the truth. He who desireth true and eternal glory careth not for that which is temporal; and he who seeketh temporal glory, or who despiseth it from his heart, is proved to bear little love for that which is heavenly. He who careth for neither praises nor reproaches hath great tranquillity of heart.

3. He will easily be contented and filled with peace, whose conscience is pure. Thou art none the holier if thou art praised, nor the viler if thou art reproached. Thou art what thou art; and thou canst not be better than God pronounceth thee to be. If thou considerest well what thou art inwardly, thou wilt not care what men will say to thee. Man looketh on the outward appearance, but the Lord looketh on the heart:(2) man looketh on the deed, but God considereth the intent. It is the token of a humble spirit always to do well, and to set little by oneself. Not to look for consolation from any created thing is a sign of great purity and inward faithfulness.

4. He that seeketh no outward witness on his own behalf, showeth plainly that he hath committed himself wholly to God. For not he that commendeth himself is approved, as St. Paul saith, but whom the Lord commendeth.(3) To walk inwardly with God, and not to be held by any outer affections, is the state of a spiritual man.

(1) Isaiah lvii. 21.   (2) 1 Samuel xvi. 7.
(3) 2 Corinthians x. 18.

CHAPTER VII

Of loving Jesus above all things

Blessed is he who understandeth what it is to love Jesus, and to despise himself for Jesus' sake. He must give up all that he loveth for his Beloved, for Jesus will be loved alone above all things. The love of created things is deceiving and unstable, but the love of Jesus is faithful and lasting. He who cleaveth to created things will fall with their slipperiness; but he who embraceth Jesus will stand upright for ever. Love Him and hold Him for thy friend, for He will not forsake thee when all depart from thee, nor will he suffer thee to perish at the last. Thou must one day be separated from all, whether thou wilt or wilt not.

2. Cleave thou to Jesus in life and death, and commit thyself unto His faithfulness, who, when all men fail thee, is alone able to help thee. Thy Beloved is such, by nature, that He will suffer no rival, but alone will possess thy heart, and as a king will sit upon His own throne. If thou wouldst learn to put away from thee every created thing, Jesus would freely take up His abode with thee. Thou wilt find all trust little better than lost which thou hast placed in men, and not in Jesus. Trust not nor lean upon a reed shaken with the wind, because all flesh is grass, and the goodliness thereof falleth as the flower of the field.(1)

3. Thou wilt be quickly deceived if thou lookest only upon the outward appearance of men, for if thou seekest thy comfort and

profit in others, thou shalt too often experience loss. If thou seekest Jesus in all things thou shalt verily find Jesus, but if thou seekest thyself thou shalt also find thyself, but to thine own hurt. For if a man seeketh not Jesus he is more hurtful to himself than all the world and all his adversaries.

(1) Isaiah xl. 6.

CHAPTER VIII

Of the intimate love of Jesus

When Jesus is present all is well and nothing seemeth hard, but when Jesus is not present everything is hard. When Jesus speaketh not within, our comfort is nothing worth, but if Jesus speaketh but a single word great is the comfort we experience. Did not Mary Magdalene rise up quickly from the place where she wept when Martha said to her, The Master is come and calleth for thee?(1) Happy hour when Jesus calleth thee from tears to the joy of the spirit! How dry and hard art thou without Jesus! How senseless and vain if thou desirest aught beyond Jesus! Is not this greater loss than if thou shouldst lose the whole world?

2. What can the world profit thee without Jesus? To be without Jesus is the nethermost hell, and to be with Jesus is sweet paradise. If Jesus were with thee no enemy could hurt thee. He who findeth Jesus findeth a good treasure, yea, good above all good; and he who loseth Jesus loseth exceeding much, yea, more than the whole world. Most poor is he who liveth without Jesus, and most rich is he who is much with Jesus.

3. It is great skill to know how to live with Jesus, and to know how to hold Jesus is great wisdom. Be thou humble and peaceable and Jesus shall be with thee. Be godly and quiet, and Jesus will remain with thee. Thou canst quickly drive away Jesus and lose His favour if thou wilt turn away to the outer things. And if thou hast put Him to flight and lost Him, to whom wilt thou flee, and whom then wilt thou seek for a friend? Without a friend thou canst not live long, and if Jesus be not thy friend above all thou shalt be very sad and desolate. Madly therefore doest thou

if thou trusteth or findest joy in any other. It is preferable
to have the whole world against thee, than Jesus offended with
thee. Therefore of all that are dear to thee, let Jesus be
specially loved.

4. Let all be loved for Jesus' sake, but Jesus for His own.
Jesus Christ alone is to be specially loved, for He alone is
found good and faithful above all friends. For His sake and in
Him let both enemies and friends be dear to thee, and pray for
them all that they may all know and love Him. Never desire to be
specially praised or loved, because this belongeth to God alone,
who hath none like unto Himself. Nor wish thou that any one set
his heart on thee, nor do thou give thyself up to the love of
any, but let Jesus be in thee and in every good man.

5. Be pure and free within thyself, and be not entangled by any
created thing. Thou oughtest to bring a bare and clean heart to
God, if thou desirest to be ready to see how gracious the Lord
is. And in truth, unless thou be prevented and drawn on by His
grace, thou wilt not attain to this, that having cast out and
dismissed all else, thou alone art united to God. For when the
grace of God cometh to a man, then he becometh able to do all
things, and when it departeth then he will be poor and weak and
given up unto troubles. In these thou art not to be cast down
nor to despair, but to rest with calm mind on the will of God,
and to bear all things which come upon thee unto the praise of
Jesus Christ; for after winter cometh summer, after night
returneth day, after the tempest a great calm.

(1) John xi. 28.

CHAPTER IX

Of the lack of all comfort

It is no hard thing to despise human comfort when divine is
present. It is a great thing, yea very great, to be able to bear
the loss both of human and divine comfort; and for the love of
God willingly to bear exile of heart, and in nought to seek
oneself, nor to look to one's own merit. What great matter is

it, if thou be cheerful of heart and devout when favour cometh to thee? That is an hour wherein all rejoice. Pleasantly enough doth he ride whom the grace of God carrieth. And what marvel, if he feeleth no burden who is carried by the Almighty, and is led onwards by the Guide from on high?

2. We are willing to accept anything for comfort, and it is difficult for a man to be freed from himself. The holy martyr Laurence overcame the love of the world and even of his priestly master, because he despised everything in the world which seemed to be pleasant; and for the love of Christ he calmly suffered even God's chief priest, Sixtus, whom he dearly loved, to be taken from him. Thus by the love of the Creator he overcame the love of man, and instead of human comfort he chose rather God's good pleasure. So also learn thou to resign any near and beloved friend for the love of God. Nor take it amiss when thou hast been deserted by a friend, knowing that we must all be parted from one another at last.

3. Mightily and long must a man strive within himself before he learn altogether to overcome himself, and to draw his whole affection towards God. When a man resteth upon himself, he easily slippeth away unto human comforts. But a true lover of Christ, and a diligent seeker after virtue, falleth not back upon those comforts, nor seeketh such sweetness as may be tasted and handled, but desireth rather hard exercises, and to undertake severe labours for Christ.

4. When, therefore, spiritual comfort is given by God, receive it with giving of thanks, and know that it is the gift of God, not thy desert. Be not lifted up, rejoice not overmuch nor foolishly presume, but rather be more humble for the gift, more wary and more careful in all thy doings; for that hour will pass away, and temptation will follow. When comfort is taken from thee, do not straightway despair, but wait for the heavenly visitation with humility and patience, for God is able to give thee back greater favour and consolation. This is not new nor strange to those who have made trial of the way of God, for with the great saints and the ancient prophets there was often this manner of change.

5. Wherefore one said when the favour of God was present with

him, I said in my prosperity I shall never be moved,(1) but he goeth on to say what he felt within himself when the favour departed: Thou didst turn Thy face from me, and I was troubled. In spite whereof he in no wise despaireth, but the more instantly entreateth God, and saith, Unto Thee, O Lord, will I cry, and will pray unto my God; and then he receiveth the fruit of his prayer, and testifieth how he hath been heard, saying, The Lord heard me and had mercy upon me, the Lord was my helper. But wherein? Thou hast turned my heaviness into joy, Thou hast put off my sackcloth and girded me with gladness. If it was thus with the great saints, we who are poor and needy ought not to despair if we are sometimes in the warmth and sometimes in the cold, for the Spirit cometh and goeth according to the good pleasure of His will. Wherefore holy Job saith, Thou dost visit him in the morning, and suddenly Thou dost prove him.(2)

6. Whereupon then can I hope, or wherein may I trust, save only in the great mercy of God, and the hope of heavenly grace? For whether good men are with me, godly brethren or faithful friends, whether holy books or beautiful discourses, whether sweet hymns and songs, all these help but little, and have but little savour when I am deserted by God's favour and left to mine own poverty. There is no better remedy, then, than patience and denial of self, and an abiding in the will of God.

7. I have never found any man so religious and godly, but that he felt sometimes a withdrawal of the divine favour, and lack of fervour. No saint was ever so filled with rapture, so enlightened, but that sooner or later he was tempted. For he is not worthy of the great vision of God, who, for God's sake, hath not been exercised by some temptation. For temptation is wont to go before as a sign of the comfort which shall follow, and heavenly comfort is promised to those who are proved by temptation. As it is written, To him that overcometh I will give to eat of the tree of life.(3)

8. Divine comfort is given that a man may be stronger to bear adversities. And temptation followeth, lest he be lifted up because of the benefit. The devil sleepeth not; thy flesh is not yet dead; therefore, cease thou not to make thyself ready unto the battle, for enemies stand on thy right hand and on thy left,

and they are never at rest.

(1) Psalm xxx. 6. (2) Job vii. 18. (3) Revelation ii. 7.

CHAPTER X

Of gratitude for the Grace of God

Why seekest thou rest when thou art born to labour? Prepare thyself for patience more than for comforts, and for bearing the cross more than for joy. For who among the men of this world would not gladly receive consolation and spiritual joy if he might always have it? For spiritual comforts exceed all the delights of the world, and all the pleasures of the flesh. For all worldly delights are either empty or unclean, whilst spiritual delights alone are pleasant and honourable, the offspring of virtue, and poured forth by God into pure minds. But no man can always enjoy these divine comforts at his own will, because the season of temptation ceaseth not for long.

2. Great is the difference between a visitation from above and false liberty of spirit and great confidence in self. God doeth well in giving us the grace of comfort, but man doeth ill in not immediately giving God thanks thereof. And thus the gifts of grace are not able to flow unto us, because we are ungrateful to the Author of them, and return them not wholly to the Fountain whence they flow. For grace ever becometh the portion of him who is grateful and that is taken away from the proud, which is wont to be given to the humble.

3. I desire no consolation which taketh away from me compunction, I love no contemplation which leadeth to pride. For all that is high is not holy, nor is everything that is sweet good; every desire is not pure; nor is everything that is dear to us pleasing unto God. Willingly do I accept that grace whereby I am made humbler and more wary and more ready to renounce myself. He who is made learned by the gift of grace and taught wisdom by the stroke of the withdrawal thereof, will not dare to claim any good thing for himself, but will rather confess that he is poor and needy. Give unto God the thing which is God's,(1) and ascribe to

thyself that which is thine; that is, give thanks unto God for
His grace, but for thyself alone confess thy fault, and that thy
punishment is deserved for thy fault.

4. Sit thou down always in the lowest room and thou shalt be
given the highest place.(2) For the highest cannot be without
the lowest. For the highest saints of God are least in their own
sight, and the more glorious they are, so much the lowlier are
they in themselves; full of grace and heavenly glory, they are
not desirous of vain-glory; resting on God and strong in His
might, they cannot be lifted up in any wise. And they who
ascribe unto God all the good which they have received, "seek not
glory one of another, but the glory which cometh from God only,"
and they desire that God shall be praised in Himself and in all
His Saints above all things, and they are always striving for
this very thing.

5. Be thankful, therefore, for the least benefit and thou shalt
be worthy to receive greater. Let the least be unto thee even as
the greatest, and let that which is of little account be unto
thee as a special gift. If the majesty of the Giver be
considered, nothing that is given shall seem small and of no
worth, for that is not a small thing which is given by the Most
High God. Yea, though He gave punishment and stripes, we ought
to be thankful, because He ever doth for our profit whatever He
suffereth to come upon us. He who seeketh to retain the favour
of God, let him be thankful for the favour which is given, and
patient in respect of that which is taken away. Let him pray
that it may return; let him be wary and humble that he lose it
not.

(1) Matthew xxii. 21.   (2) Luke xiv. 10.

CHAPTER XI

Of the fewness of those who love the Cross of Jesus

Jesus hath many lovers of His heavenly kingdom, but few bearers of
His Cross. He hath many seekers of comfort, but few of
tribulation. He findeth many companions of His table, but few of

His fasting. All desire to rejoice with Him, few are willing to undergo anything for His sake. Many follow Jesus that they may eat of His loaves, but few that they may drink of the cup of His passion. Many are astonished at His Miracles, few follow after the shame of His Cross. Many love Jesus so long as no adversities happen to them. Many praise Him and bless Him, so long as they receive any comforts from Him. But if Jesus hide Himself and withdraw from them a little while, they fall either into complaining or into too great dejection of mind.

2. But they who love Jesus for Jesus' sake, and not for any consolation of their own, bless Him in all tribulation and anguish of heart as in the highest consolation. And if He should never give them consolation, nevertheless they would always praise Him and always give Him thanks.

3. Oh what power hath the pure love of Jesus, unmixed with any gain or love of self! Should not all they be called mercenary who are always seeking consolations? Do they not prove themselves lovers of self more than of Christ who are always seeking their own gain and advantage? Where shall be found one who is willing to serve God altogether for nought?

4. Rarely is any one found so spiritual as to be stripped of all selfish thoughts, for who shall find a man truly poor in spirit and free of all created things? "His value is from afar, yea from the ends of the earth." A man may give away all his goods, yet that is nothing; and if he do many deeds of penitence, yet that is a small thing; and though he understand all knowledge, yet that is afar off; and if he have great virtue and zealous devotion, yet much is lacking unto him, yea, one thing which is the most necessary to him of all. What is it then? That having given up all things besides, he give up himself and go forth from himself utterly, and retain nothing of self-love; and having done all things which he knoweth to be his duty to do, that he feel that he hath done nothing. Let him not reckon that much which might be much esteemed, but let him pronounce himself to be in truth an unprofitable servant, as the Truth Himself saith, When ye have done all things that are commanded you, say, we are unprofitable servants.(1) Then may he be truly poor and naked in spirit, and be able to say with the Prophet, As for me, I am poor

and needy.(2) Nevertheless, no man is richer than he, no man stronger, no man freer. For he knoweth both how to give up himself and all things, and how to be lowly in his own eyes.

(1) Luke xvii. 10.   (2) Psalm xxv. 16.

CHAPTER XII

Of the royal way of the Holy Cross

That seemeth a hard saying to many, If any man will come after Me, let him deny himself and take up his Cross and follow Me.(1) But it will be much harder to hear that last sentence, Depart from me, ye wicked, into eternal fire.(2) For they who now willingly hear the word of the Cross and follow it, shall not then fear the hearing of eternal damnation. This sign of the Cross shall be in heaven when the Lord cometh to Judgment. Then all servants of the Cross, who in life have conformed themselves to the Crucified, shall draw nigh unto Christ the Judge with great boldness.

2. Why fearest thou then to take up the cross which leadeth to a kingdom? In the Cross is health, in the Cross is life, in the Cross is protection from enemies, in the Cross is heavenly sweetness, in the Cross strength of mind, in the Cross joy of the spirit, in the Cross the height of virtue, in the Cross perfection of holiness. There is no health of the soul, no hope of eternal life, save in the Cross. Take up therefore, thy cross and follow Jesus and thou shalt go into eternal life. He went before thee bearing His Cross and died for thee upon the Cross, that thou also mayest bear thy cross and mayest love to be crucified upon it. For if thou be dead with Him, thou shalt also live with Him, and if thou be a partaker of His sufferings thou shalt be also of His glory.

3. Behold everything dependeth upon the Cross, and everything lieth in dying; and there is none other way unto life and to true inward peace, except the way of the Holy Cross and of daily mortification. Go where thou wilt, seek whatsoever thou wilt, and thou shalt find no higher way above nor safer way below, than

the way of the Holy Cross. Dispose and order all things
according to thine own will and judgment, and thou shalt ever
find something to suffer either willingly or unwillingly, and
thus thou shalt ever find thy cross. For thou shalt either feel
pain of body, or tribulation of spirit within thy soul.

4. Sometimes thou wilt be forsaken of God, sometimes thou wilt be
tried by thy neighbour, and which is more, thou wilt often be
wearisome to thyself. And still thou canst not be delivered nor
eased by any remedy or consolation, but must bear so long as God
will. For God will have thee learn to suffer tribulation without
consolation, and to submit thyself fully to it, and by
tribulation be made more humble. No man understandeth the
Passion of Christ in his heart so well as he who hath had
somewhat of the like suffering himself. The Cross therefore is
always ready, and every where waiteth for thee. Thou canst not
flee from it whithersoever thou hurriest, for whithersoever thou
comest, thou bearest thyself with thee, and shalt ever find
thyself. Turn thee above, turn thee below, turn thee without,
turn thee within, and in them all thou shalt find the Cross; and
needful is it that thou everywhere possess patience if thou wilt
have internal peace and gain the everlasting crown.

5. If thou willingly bear the Cross, it will bear thee, and will
bring thee to the end which thou seekest, even where there shall
be the end of suffering; though it shall not be here. If thou
bear it unwillingly, thou makest a burden for thyself and greatly
increaseth thy load, and yet thou must bear it. If thou cast
away one cross, without doubt thou shalt find another and
perchance a heavier.

6. Thinketh thou to escape what no mortal hath been able to
avoid? Which of the saints in the world hath been without the
cross and tribulation? For not even Jesus Christ our Lord was
one hour without the anguish of His Passion, so long as He lived.
It behooved, He said, Christ to suffer and to rise from the dead,
and so enter into his glory.(3) And how dost thou seek another
way than this royal way, which is the way of the Holy Cross?

7. The whole life of Christ was a cross and martyrdom, and dost
thou seek for thyself rest and joy? Thou art wrong, thou art

wrong, if thou seekest aught but to suffer tribulations, for this whole mortal life is full of miseries, and set round with crosses. And the higher a man hath advanced in the spirit, the heavier crosses he will often find, because the sorrow of his banishment increaseth with the strength of his love.

8. But yet the man who is thus in so many wise afflicted, is not without refreshment of consolation, because he feeleth abundant fruit to be growing within him out of the bearing of his cross. For whilst he willingly submitteth himself to it, every burden of tribulation is turned into an assurance of divine comfort, and the more the flesh is wasted by affliction, the more is the spirit strengthened mightily by inward grace. And ofttimes so greatly is he comforted by the desire for tribulation and adversity, through love of conformity to the Cross of Christ, that he would not be without sorrow and tribulation; for he believeth that he shall be the more acceptable to God, the more and the heavier burdens he is able to bear for His sake. This is not the virtue of man, but the grace of Christ which hath such power and energy in the weak flesh, that what it naturally hateth and fleeth from, this it draweth to and loveth through fervour of spirit.

9. It is not in the nature of man to bear the cross, to love the cross, to keep under the body and to bring it into subjection, to fly from honours, to bear reproaches meekly, to despise self and desire to be despised, to bear all adversities and losses, and to desire no prosperity in this world. If thou lookest to thyself, thou wilt of thyself be able to do none of this; but if thou trustest in the Lord, endurance shall be given thee from heaven, and the world and the flesh shall be made subject to thy command. Yea, thou shalt not even fear thine adversary the devil, if thou be armed with faith and signed with the Cross of Christ.

10. Set thyself, therefore, like a good and faithful servant of Christ, to the manful bearing of the Cross of thy Lord, who out of love was crucified for thee. Prepare thyself for the bearing many adversities and manifold troubles in this wretched life; because so it shall be with thee wheresoever thou art, and so in very deed thou shalt find it, wherever thou hide thyself. This it must be; and there is no means of escaping from tribulation

and sorrow, except to bear them patiently. Drink thou lovingly
thy Lord's cup if thou desirest to be His friend and to have thy
lot with Him. Leave consolations to God, let Him do as seemeth
best to Him concerning them. But do thou set thyself to endure
tribulations, and reckon them the best consolations; for the
sufferings of this present time are not worthy to be compared
with the glory which shall be revealed in us,(4) nor would they
be even if thou wert to endure them all.

11. When thou hast come to this, that tribulation is sweet and
pleasant to thee for Christ's sake, then reckon that it is well
with thee, because thou hast found paradise on earth. So long as
it is hard to thee to suffer and thou desirest to escape, so long
it will not be well with thee, and tribulations will follow thee
everywhere.

12. If thou settest thyself to that thou oughtest, namely, to
suffer and to die, it shall soon go better with thee, and thou
shalt find peace. Though thou shouldest be caught up with Paul
unto the third heaven,(5) thou art not on that account secure
from suffering evil. I will show him, saith Jesus, what great
things he must suffer for My Name's sake.(6) It remaineth,
therefore, to thee to suffer, if thou wilt love Jesus and serve
Him continually.

13. Oh that thou wert worthy to suffer something for the name of
Jesus, how great glory should await thee, what rejoicing among
all the saints of God, what bright example also to thy neighbour!
For all men commend patience, although few be willing to practise
it. Thou oughtest surely to suffer a little for Christ when many
suffer heavier things for the world.

14. Know thou of a surety that thou oughtest to lead the life of
a dying man. And the more a man dieth to himself, the more he
beginneth to live towards God. None is fit for the understanding
of heavenly things, unless he hath submitted himself to bearing
adversities for Christ. Nothing more acceptable to God, nothing
more healthful for thyself in this world, than to suffer
willingly for Christ. And if it were thine to choose, thou
oughtest rather to wish to suffer adversities for Christ, than to
be refreshed with manifold consolations, for thou wouldest be

more like Christ and more conformed to all saints. For our worthiness and growth in grace lieth not in many delights and consolations, but rather in bearing many troubles and adversities.

15. If indeed there had been anything better and more profitable to the health of men than to suffer, Christ would surely have shown it by word and example. For both the disciples who followed Him, and all who desire to follow Him, He plainly exhorteth to bear their cross, and saith, If any man will come after Me, let him deny himself and take up his cross, and follow Me.(7) So now that we have thoroughly read and studied all things, let us hear the conclusion of the whole matter. We must through much tribulation enter into the kingdom of God.(8)

(1) Matthew xvi. 24. (2) Matthew xxv. 41. (3) Luke xxiv. 46.
(4) Romans viii. 18. (5) 2 Corinthians xii. 2.
(6) Acts ix. 16. (7) Luke ix. 23. (8) Acts xiv. 21.

THE THIRD BOOK

ON INWARD CONSOLATION

CHAPTER I

Of the inward voice of Christ to the faithful soul

I will hearken what the Lord God shall say within me.(1) Blessed is the soul which heareth the Lord speaking within it, and receiveth the word of consolation from His mouth. Blessed are the ears which receive the echoes of the soft whisper of God, and turn not aside to the whisperings of this world. Blessed truly are the ears which listen not to the voice that soundeth without, but to that which teacheth truth inwardly. Blessed are the eyes which are closed to things without, but are fixed upon things within. Blessed are they who search inward things and study to prepare themselves more and more by daily exercises for the receiving of heavenly mysteries. Blessed are they who long to have leisure for God, and free themselves from every hindrance of the world. Think on these things, O my soul, and shut the doors of thy carnal desires, so mayest thou hear what the Lord God will say within thee.

2. These things saith thy Beloved, "I am thy salvation, I am thy peace and thy life. Keep thee unto Me, and thou shalt find peace." Put away thee all transitory things, seek those things that are eternal. For what are all temporal things but deceits, and what shall all created things help thee if thou be forsaken by the Creator? Therefore put all things else away, and give thyself to the Creator, to be well pleasing and faithful to Him, that thou mayest be able to attain true blessedness.

(1) Psalm lxxxv. 8.

CHAPTER II

What the truth saith inwardly without noise of words

Speak Lord, for thy servant heareth.(1) I am Thy servant; O give me understanding that I may know Thy testimonies. Incline my heart unto the words of Thy mouth.(2) Let thy speech distil as the dew. The children of Israel spake in old time to Moses, Speak thou unto us and we will hear, but let not the Lord speak unto us lest we die.(3) Not thus, O Lord, not thus do I pray, but rather with Samuel the prophet, I beseech Thee humbly and earnestly, Speak, Lord, for Thy servant heareth. Let not Moses speak to me, nor any prophet, but rather speak Thou, O Lord, who didst inspire and illuminate all the prophets; for Thou alone without them canst perfectly fill me with knowledge, whilst they without Thee shall profit nothing.

2. They can indeed utter words, but they give not the spirit. They speak with exceeding beauty, but when Thou art silent they kindle not the heart. They give us scriptures, but Thou makest known the sense thereof. They bring us mysteries, but Thou revealest the things which are signified. They utter

commandments, but Thou helpest to the fulfilling of them. They show the way, but Thou givest strength for the journey. They act only outwardly, but Thou dost instruct and enlighten the heart. They water, but Thou givest the increase. They cry with words, but Thou givest understanding to the hearer.

3. Therefore let not Moses speak to me, but Thou, O Lord my God, Eternal Truth; lest I die and bring forth no fruit, being outwardly admonished, but not enkindled within; lest the word heard but not followed, known but not loved, believed but not obeyed, rise up against me in the judgment. Speak, Lord, for Thy servant heareth; Thou hast the words of eternal life.(4) Speak unto me for some consolation unto my soul, for the amendment of my whole life, and for the praise and glory and eternal honour of Thy Name.

(1) 1 Samuel iii. 9.   (2) Psalm cxix. 125.   (3) Exodus xx. 19.
(4) John vi. 68.

CHAPTER III

How all the words of God are to be heard with humility, and how many consider them not

"My Son, hear My words, for My words are most sweet, surpassing all the knowledge of the philosophers and wise men of this world. My words are spirit, and they are life,(1) and are not to be weighed by man's understanding. They are not to be drawn forth for vain approbation, but to be heard in silence, and to be received with all humility and with deep love."

2. And I said, "Blessed is the man whom Thou teachest, O Lord, and instructest him in Thy law, that Thou mayest give him rest in time of adversity,(2) and that he be not desolate in the earth."

3. "I," saith the Lord, "taught the prophets from the beginning, and even now cease I not to speak unto all; but many are deaf and hardened against My voice; many love to listen to the world rather than to God, they follow after the desires of the flesh more readily than after the good pleasure of God. The world

promiseth things that are temporal and small, and it is served with great eagerness. I promise things that are great and eternal, and the hearts of mortals are slow to stir. Who serveth and obeyeth Me in all things, with such carefulness as he serveth the world and its rulers?

> Be thou ashamed, O Sidon, saith the sea;(3)
> And if thou reason seekest, hear thou me.

For a little reward men make a long journey; for eternal life many will scarce lift a foot once from the ground. Mean reward is sought after; for a single piece of money sometimes there is shameful striving; for a thing which is vain and for a trifling promise, men shrink not from toiling day and night."

4. "But, O shame! for an unchangeable good, for an inestimable reward, for the highest honour and for a glory that fadeth not away, it is irksome to them to toil even a little. Be thou ashamed therefore, slothful and discontented servant, for they are found readier unto perdition than thou unto life. They rejoice more heartily in vanity than thou in the truth. Sometimes, indeed, they are disappointed of their hope, but my promise faileth no man, nor sendeth away empty him who trusteth in Me. What I have promised I will give; what I have said I will fulfil; if only a man remain faithful in My love unto the end. Therefore am I the rewarder of all good men, and a strong approver of all who are godly.

5. "Write My words in thy heart and consider them diligently, for they shall be very needful to thee in time of temptation. What thou understandest not when thou readest, thou shalt know in the time of thy visitation. I am wont to visit Mine elect in twofold manner, even by temptation and by comfort, and I teach them two lessons day by day, the one in chiding their faults, the other in exhorting them to grow in grace. He who hath My words and rejecteth them, hath one who shall judge him at the last day."

A PRAYER FOR THE SPIRIT OF DEVOTION

6. O Lord my God, Thou art all my good, and who am I that I should dare to speak unto Thee? I am the very poorest of Thy servants, an abject worm, much poorer and more despicable than I know or dare to say. Nevertheless remember, O Lord, that I am nothing, I have nothing, and can do nothing. Thou only art good, just and holy; Thou canst do all things, art over all things, fillest all things, leaving empty only the sinner. Call to mind Thy tender mercies, and fill my heart with Thy grace, Thou who wilt not that Thy work should return to Thee void.

7. How can I bear this miserable life unless Thy mercy and grace strengthen me? Turn not away Thy face from me, delay not Thy visitation. Withdraw not Thou Thy comfort from me, lest my soul "gasp after thee as a thirsty land." Lord, teach me to do Thy will, teach me to walk humbly and uprightly before Thee, for Thou art my wisdom, who knowest me in truth, and knewest me before the world was made and before I was born into the world.

(1) John vi. 63.   (2) Psalm xciv. 13.   (3) Isaiah xxiii. 4.

CHAPTER IV

How we must walk in truth and humility before God

"My Son! walk before Me in truth, and in the simplicity of thy heart seek Me continually. He who walketh before Me in the truth shall be safe from evil assaults, and the truth shall deliver him from the wiles and slanders of the wicked. If the truth shall make thee free, thou shalt be free indeed, and shalt not care for the vain words of men."

2. Lord, it is true as Thou sayest; let it, I pray Thee, be so with me; let Thy truth teach me, let it keep me and preserve me safe unto the end. Let it free me from all evil and inordinate affection, and I will walk before Thee in great freedom of heart.

3. "I will teach thee," saith the Truth, "the things which are right and pleasing before Me. Think upon thy sins with great

displeasure and sorrow, and never think thyself anything because of thy good works. Verily thou art a sinner, liable to many passions, yea, tied and bound with them. Of thyself thou always tendest unto nothing, thou wilt quickly fall, quickly be conquered, quickly disturbed, quickly undone. Thou hast nought whereof to glory, but many reasons why thou shouldest reckon thyself vile, for thou art far weaker than thou art able to comprehend.

4. "Let, therefore, nothing which thou doest seem to thee great; let nothing be grand, nothing of value or beauty, nothing worthy of honour, nothing lofty, nothing praiseworthy or desirable, save what is eternal. Let the eternal truth please thee above all things, let thine own great vileness displease thee continually. Fear, denounce, flee nothing so much as thine own faults and sins, which ought to be more displeasing to thee than any loss whatsoever of goods. There are some who walk not sincerely before me, but being led by curiosity and pride, they desire to know my secret things and to understand the deep things of God, whilst they neglect themselves and their salvation. These often fall into great temptations and sins because of their pride and curiosity, for I am against them.

5. "Fear thou the judgments of God, fear greatly the wrath of the Almighty. Shrink from debating upon the works of the Most High, but search narrowly thine own iniquities into what great sins thou hast fallen, and how many good things thou hast neglected. There are some who carry their devotion only in books, some in pictures, some in outward signs and figures; some have Me in their mouths, but little in their hearts. Others there are who, being enlightened in their understanding and purged in their affections, continually long after eternal things, hear of earthly things with unwillingness, obey the necessities of nature with sorrow. And these understand what the Spirit of truth speaketh in them; for He teacheth them to despise earthly things and to love heavenly; to neglect the world and to desire heaven all the day and night."

CHAPTER V

Of the wonderful power of the Divine Love

I bless Thee, O Heavenly Father, Father of my Lord Jesus Christ, for that Thou hast vouchsafed to think of me, poor that I am. O, Father of Mercies and God of all comfort,(1) I give thanks unto Thee, who refreshest me sometimes with thine own comfort, when I am unworthy of any comfort. I bless and glorify Thee continually, with thine only begotten Son and the Holy Ghost, the Paraclete, for ever and ever. O Lord God, Holy lover of my soul, when Thou shalt come into my heart, all my inward parts shall rejoice. Thou art my glory and the joy of my heart. Thou art my hope and my refuge in the day of my trouble.

2. But because I am still weak in love and imperfect in virtue, I need to be strengthened and comforted by Thee; therefore visit Thou me often and instruct me with Thy holy ways of discipline. Deliver me from evil passions, and cleanse my heart from all inordinate affections, that, being healed and altogether cleansed within, I may be made ready to love, strong to suffer, steadfast to endure.

3. Love is a great thing, a good above all others, which alone maketh every heavy burden light, and equaliseth every inequality. For it beareth the burden and maketh it no burden, it maketh every bitter thing to be sweet and of good taste. The surpassing love of Jesus impelleth to great works, and exciteth to the continual desiring of greater perfection. Love willeth to be raised up, and not to be held down by any mean thing. Love willeth to be free and aloof from all worldly affection, lest its inward power of vision be hindered, lest it be entangled by any worldly prosperity or overcome by adversity. Nothing is sweeter than love, nothing stronger, nothing loftier, nothing broader, nothing pleasanter, nothing fuller or better in heaven nor on earth, for love was born of God and cannot rest save in God above all created things.

4. He who loveth flyeth, runneth, and is glad; he is free and not hindered. He giveth all things for all things, and hath all things in all things, because he resteth in One who is high above

all, from whom every good floweth and proceedeth. He looketh not for gifts, but turneth himself to the Giver above all good things. Love oftentimes knoweth no measure, but breaketh out above all measure; love feeleth no burden, reckoneth not labours, striveth after more than it is able to do, pleadeth not impossibility, because it judgeth all things which are lawful for it to be possible. It is strong therefore for all things, and it fulfilleth many things, and is successful where he who loveth not faileth and lieth down.

5. Love is watchful, and whilst sleeping still keepeth watch; though fatigued it is not weary, though pressed it is not forced, though alarmed it is not terrified, but like the living flame and the burning torch, it breaketh forth on high and securely triumpheth. If a man loveth, he knoweth what this voice crieth. For the ardent affection of the soul is a great clamour in the ears of God, and it saith: My God, my Beloved! Thou art all mine, and I am all Thine.

6. Enlarge Thou me in love, that I may learn to taste with the innermost mouth of my heart how sweet it is to love, to be dissolved, and to swim in love. Let me be holden by love, mounting above myself through exceeding fervour and admiration. Let me sing the song of love, let me follow Thee my Beloved on high, let my soul exhaust itself in Thy praise, exulting with love. Let me love Thee more than myself, not loving myself except for Thy sake, and all men in Thee who truly love Thee, as the law of love commandeth which shineth forth from Thee.

7. Love is swift, sincere, pious, pleasant, gentle, strong, patient, faithful, prudent, long-suffering, manly, and never seeking her own; for wheresoever a man seeketh his own, there he falleth from love. Love is circumspect, humble, and upright; not weak, not fickle, nor intent on vain things; sober, chaste, steadfast, quiet, and guarded in all the senses. Love is subject and obedient to all that are in authority, vile and lowly in its own sight, devout and grateful towards God, faithful and always trusting in Him even when God hideth His face, for without sorrow we cannot live in love.

8. He who is not ready to suffer all things, and to conform to

the will of the Beloved, is not worthy to be called a lover of God. It behoveth him who loveth to embrace willingly all hard and bitter things for the Beloved's sake, and not to be drawn away from Him because of any contrary accidents.

(1) 2 Corinthians i. 3.

CHAPTER VI

Of the proving of the true lover

"My Son, thou art not yet strong and prudent in thy love."

2. Wherefore, O my Lord?

3. "Because for a little opposition thou fallest away from thy undertakings, and too eagerly seekest after consolation. The strong lover standeth fast in temptations, and believeth not the evil persuasions of the enemy. As in prosperity I please him, so in adversity I do not displease.

4. "The prudent lover considereth not the gift of the lover so much as the love of the giver. He looketh for the affection more than the value, and setteth all gifts lower than the Beloved. The noble lover resteth not in the gift, but in Me above every gift.

5. "All is not lost, though thou sometimes think of Me or of My saints, less than thou shouldest desire. That good and sweet affection which thou sometimes perceivest is the effect of present grace and some foretaste of the heavenly country; but hereon thou must not too much depend, for it goeth and cometh. But to strive against the evil motions of the mind which come to us, and to resist the suggestions of the devil, is a token of virtue and great merit.

6. "Therefore let not strange fancies disturb thee, whencesoever they arise. Bravely observe thy purpose and thy upright intentions towards God. It is not an illusion when thou art sometimes suddenly carried away into rapture, and then suddenly

art brought back to the wonted vanities of thy heart. For thou dost rather unwillingly undergo them than cause them; and so long as they displease thee and thou strivest against them, it is a merit and no loss.

7. "Know thou that thine old enemy altogether striveth to hinder thy pursuit after good, and to deter thee from every godly exercise, to wit, the contemplation of the Saints, the pious remembrance of My passion, the profitable recollection of sin, the keeping of thy own heart, and the steadfast purpose to grow in virtue. He suggesteth to thee many evil thoughts, that he may work in thee weariness and terror, and so draw thee away from prayer and holy reading. Humble confession displeaseth him, and if he were able he would make thee to cease from Communion. Believe him not, nor heed him, though many a time he hath laid for thee the snares of deceit. Account it to be from him, when he suggesteth evil and unclean thoughts. Say unto him, 'Depart unclean spirit; put on shame, miserable one; horribly unclean art thou, who bringest such things to mine ears. Depart from me, detestable deceiver; thou shalt have no part in me; but Jesus shall be with me, as a strong warrior, and thou shalt stand confounded. Rather would I die and bear all suffering, than consent unto thee. Hold thy peace and be dumb; I will not hear thee more, though thou plottest more snares against me. The Lord is my light and my salvation: whom then shall I fear? Though a host of men should rise up against me, yet shall not my heart be afraid. The Lord is my strength and my Redeemer.'(1)

8. "Strive thou like a good soldier; and if sometimes thou fail through weakness, put on thy strength more bravely than before, trusting in My more abundant grace, and take thou much heed of vain confidence and pride. Because of it many are led into error, and sometimes fall into blindness well-nigh irremediable. Let this ruin of the proud, who foolishly lift themselves up, be to thee for a warning and a continual exhortation to humility."

(1) Psalms xxvii. 1-3; xix. 14.

CHAPTER VII

Of hiding our grace under the guard of humility

"My Son, it is better and safer for thee to hide the grace of devotion, and not to lift thyself up on high, nor to speak much thereof, nor to value it greatly; but rather to despise thyself, and to fear as though this grace were given to one unworthy thereof. Nor must thou depend too much upon this feeling, for it can very quickly be turned into its opposite. Think when thou art in a state of grace how miserable and poor thou art wont to be without grace. Nor is there advance in spiritual life in this alone, that thou hast the grace of consolation, but that thou humbly and unselfishly and patiently takest the withdrawal thereof; so that thou cease not from the exercise of prayer, nor suffer thy other common duties to be in anywise neglected; rather do thy task more readily, as though thou hadst gained more strength and knowledge; and do not altogether neglect thyself because of the dearth and anxiety of spirit which thou feelest.

2. "For there are many who, when things have not gone prosperous with them, become forthwith impatient or slothful. For the way of a man is not in himself,(1) but it is God's to give and to console, when He will, and as much as He will, and whom He will, as it shall please Him, and no further. Some who were presumptuous because of the grace of devotion within them, have destroyed themselves, because they would do more than they were able, not considering the measure of their own littleness, but rather following the impulse of the heart than the judgment of the reason. And because they presumed beyond what was well-pleasing unto God, therefore they quickly lost grace. They became poor and were left vile, who had built for themselves their nest in heaven; so that being humbled and stricken with poverty, they might learn not to fly with their own wings, but to put their trust under My feathers. They who are as yet new and unskilled in the way of the Lord, unless they rule themselves after the counsel of the wise, may easily be deceived and led away.

3. "But if they wish to follow their own fancies rather than trust the experience of others, the result will be very dangerous

to them if they still refuse to be drawn away from their own notion. Those who are wise in their own conceits, seldom patiently endure to be ruled by others. It is better to have a small portion of wisdom with humility, and a slender understanding, than great treasures of sciences with vain self-esteem. It is better for thee to have less than much of what may make thee proud. He doeth not very discreetly who giveth up himself entirely to joy, forgetting his former helplessness and the chaste fear of the Lord, which feareth to lose the grace offered. Nor is he very wise, after a manly sort, who in time of adversity, or any trouble whatsoever, beareth himself too despairingly, and feeleth concerning Me less trustfully than he ought.

4. "He who in time of peace willeth to be oversecure shall be often found in time of war overdispirited and full of fears. If thou knewest always how to continue humble and moderate in thyself, and to guide and rule thine own spirit well, thou wouldest not so quickly fall into danger and mischief. It is good counsel that when fervour of spirit is kindled, thou shouldest meditate how it will be with thee when the light is taken away. Which when it doth happen, remember that still the light may return again, which I have taken away for a time for a warning to thee, and also for mine own glory. Such a trial is often more useful than if thou hadst always things prosperous according to thine own will.

5. "For merits are not to be reckoned by this, that a man hath many visions or consolations, or that he is skilled in the Scriptures, or that he is placed in a high situation; but that he is grounded upon true humility and filled with divine charity, that he always purely and uprightly seeketh the honour of God, that he setteth not by himself, but unfeignedly despiseth himself, and even rejoiceth to be despised and humbled by others more than to be honoured."

(1) Jeremiah x. 23.

CHAPTER VIII

Of a low estimation of self in the sight of God

I will speak unto my Lord who am but dust and ashes. If I count myself more, behold Thou standest against me, and my iniquities bear true testimony, and I cannot gainsay it. But if I abase myself, and bring myself to nought, and shrink from all self-esteem, and grind myself to dust, which I am, Thy grace will be favourable unto me, and Thy light will be near unto my heart; and all self-esteem, how little soever it be, shall be swallowed up in the depths of my nothingness, and shall perish for ever. There Thou showest to me myself, what I am, what I was, and whither I have come: so foolish was I and ignorant.(1) If I am left to myself, behold I am nothing, I am all weakness; but if suddenly Thou look upon me, immediately I am made strong, and filled with new joy. And it is great marvel that I am so suddenly lifted up, and so graciously embraced by Thee, since I am always being carried to the deep by my own weight.

2. This is the doing of Thy love which freely goeth before me and succoureth me in so many necessities, which guardeth me also in great dangers and snatcheth me, as I may truly say, from innumerable evils. For verily, by loving myself amiss, I lost myself, and by seeking and sincerely loving Thee alone, I found both myself and Thee, and through love I have brought myself to yet deeper nothingness: because Thou, O most sweet Lord, dealest with me beyond all merit, and above all which I dare ask or think.

3. Blessed be Thou, O my God, because though I be unworthy of all Thy benefits, Thy bountiful and infinite goodness never ceaseth to do good even to ingrates and to those who are turned far from Thee. Turn Thou us unto Thyself, that we may be grateful, humble, and godly, for Thou art our salvation, our courage, and our strength.

(1) Psalm lxxiii. 22.

CHAPTER IX

That all things are to be referred to God, as the final end

"My Son, I must be thy Supreme and final end, if thou desirest to be truly happy. Out of such purpose thy affection shall be purified, which too often is sinfully bent upon itself and upon created things. For if thou seekest thyself in any matter, straightway thou wilt fail within thyself and grow barren. Therefore refer everything to Me first of all, for it is I who gave thee all. So look upon each blessing as flowing from the Supreme Good, and thus all things are to be attributed to Me as their source.

2. "From Me the humble and great, the poor and the rich, draw water as from a living fountain, and those who serve Me with a free and faithful spirit shall receive grace for grace. But he who will glory apart from Me, or will be delighted with any good which lieth in himself, shall not be established in true joy, nor shall be enlarged in heart, but shall be greatly hindered and thrown into tribulation. Therefore thou must not ascribe any good to thyself, nor look upon virtue as belonging to any man, but ascribe it all unto God, without whom man hath nothing. I gave all, I will receive all again, and with great strictness require I the giving of thanks.

3. "This is the Truth, and by it the vanity of boasting is put to flight. And if heavenly grace and true charity shall enter into thee, there shall be no envy, nor straitening of the heart, nor shall any self-love take possession of thee. For divine charity conquereth all things, and enlargeth all the powers of the soul. If thou art truly wise, thou wilt rejoice in Me alone, thou wilt hope in Me alone; for there is none good but one, that is God,[1] Who is to be praised above all things, and in all things to receive blessing."

[1] Luke xviii. 19.

CHAPTER X

That it is sweet to despise the world and to serve God

Now will I speak again, O my Lord, and hold not my peace; I will say in the ears of my God, my Lord, and my King, who is exalted above all, Oh how plentiful is Thy goodness which Thou hast laid up for them that fear Thee!(1) But what art Thou to those who love Thee? What to those who serve Thee with their whole heart? Truly unspeakable is the sweetness of the contemplation of Thee, which Thou bestowest upon those who love Thee. In this most of all Thou hast showed me the sweetness of Thy charity, that when I was not, Thou madest me, and when I wandered far from Thee, Thou broughtest me back that I might serve Thee, and commandedst me to love Thee.

2. O Fountain of perpetual love, what shall I say concerning Thee? How shall I be unmindful of Thee, who didst vouchsafe to remember me, even after I pined away and perished? Thou hast had mercy beyond all hope upon Thy servant, and hast showed Thy grace and friendship beyond all deserving. What reward shall I render Thee for this Thy grace? For it is not given unto all to renounce this world and its affairs, and to take up a religious life. For is it a great thing that I should serve Thee, whom every creature ought to serve? It ought not to seem a great thing to me to serve Thee; but rather this appeareth to me a great and wonderful thing, that Thou vouchsafest to receive as Thy servant one so poor and unworthy, and to join him unto Thy chosen servants.

3. Behold all things which I have are Thine, and with them I serve Thee. And yet verily it is Thou who servest me, rather than I Thee. Behold the heaven and the earth which Thou hast created for the service of men; they are at Thy bidding, and perform daily whatsoever Thou dost command. Yea, and this is little; for Thou hast even ordained the Angels for the service of man. But it surpasseth even all these things, that Thou Thyself didst vouchsafe to minister unto man, and didst promise that Thou wouldest give Thyself unto him.

4. What shall I render unto Thee for all these Thy manifold

mercies? Oh that I were able to serve Thee all the days of my life! Oh that even for one day I were enabled to do Thee service worthy of Thyself! For verily Thou art worthy of all service, all honour, and praise without end. Verily Thou art my God, and I am Thy poor servant, who am bound to serve Thee with all my strength, nor ought I ever to grow weary of Thy praise. This is my wish, this is my exceeding great desire, and whatsoever is lacking to me, vouchsafe Thou to supply.

5. It is great honour, great glory to serve Thee, and to despise all for Thy sake. For they shall have great grace who of their own will shall submit themselves to Thy most holy service. They who for Thy love have cast away every carnal delight shall find the sweetest consolation of the Holy Ghost. They who enter the narrow way of life for Thy Name's sake, and have put away all worldly cares, shall attain great liberty of spirit.

6. Oh grateful and delightsome service of God, whereby man is made truly free and holy! Oh sacred condition of the religious servant, which maketh man equal to the Angels, well-pleasing unto God, terrible to evil spirits, and acceptable to all faithful ones! Oh service to be embraced and ever desired, in which the highest good is promised, and joy is gained which shall remain for evermore!

(1) Psalm xxxi. 21.

CHAPTER XI

That the desires of the heart are to be examined and governed

"My Son, thou hast still many things to learn, which thou hast not well learned yet."

2. What are they, Lord?

3. "To place thy desire altogether in subjection to My good pleasure, and not to be a lover of thyself, but an earnest seeker of My will. Thy desires often excite and urge thee forward; but consider with thyself whether thou art not more moved for thine

own objects than for My honour. If it is Myself that thou seekest, thou shalt be well content with whatsoever I shall ordain; but if any pursuit of thine own lieth hidden within thee, behold it is this which hindereth and weigheth thee down.

4. "Beware, therefore, lest thou strive too earnestly after some desire which thou hast conceived, without taking counsel of Me; lest haply it repent thee afterwards, and that displease thee which before pleased, and for which thou didst long as for a great good. For not every affection which seemeth good is to be forthwith followed; neither is every opposite affection to be immediately avoided. Sometimes it is expedient to use restraint even in good desires and wishes, lest through importunity thou fall into distraction of mind, lest through want of discipline thou become a stumbling-block to others, or lest by the resistance of others thou be suddenly disturbed and brought to confusion.

5. "Sometimes, indeed, it is needful to use violence, and manfully to strive against the sensual appetite, and not to consider what the flesh may or not will; but rather to strive after this, that it may become subject, however unwillingly, to the spirit. And for so long it ought to be chastised and compelled to undergo slavery, even until it be ready for all things, and learn to be contented with little, to be delighted with things simple, and never to murmur at any inconvenience."

CHAPTER XII

Of the inward growth of patience, and of the struggle against evil desires

O Lord God, I see that patience is very necessary unto me; for many things in this life fall out contrary. For howsoever I may have contrived for my peace, my life cannot go on without strife and trouble.

2. "Thou speakest truly, My Son. For I will not that thou seek such a peace as is without trials, and knoweth no adversities; but rather that thou shouldest judge thyself to have found peace,

when thou art tried with manifold tribulations, and proved by many adversities. If thou shalt say that thou art not able to bear much, how then wilt thou sustain the fire hereafter? Of two evils we should always choose the less. Therefore, that thou mayest escape eternal torments hereafter, strive on God's behalf to endure present evils bravely. Thinkest thou that the children of this world suffer nought, or but little? Thou wilt not find it so, even though thou find out the most prosperous.

3. "'But,' thou wilt say, 'they have many delights, and they follow their own wills, and thus they bear lightly their tribulations.'

4. "Be it so, grant that they have what they list; but how long, thinkest thou, will it last? Behold, like the smoke those who are rich in this world will pass away, and no record shall remain of their past joys. Yea, even while they yet live, they rest not without bitterness and weariness and fear. For from the very same thing wherein they find delight, thence they oftentimes have the punishment of sorrow. Justly it befalleth them, that because out of measure they seek out and pursue pleasures, they enjoy them not without confusion and bitterness. Oh how short, how false, how inordinate and wicked are all these pleasures! Yet because of their sottishness and blindness men do not understand; but like brute beasts, for the sake of a little pleasure of this corruptible life, they incur death of the soul. Thou therefore, my son, go not after thy lusts, but refrain thyself from thine appetites.(1) Delight thou in the Lord, and He shall give thee thy heart's desire.(2)

5. "For if thou wilt truly find delight, and be abundantly comforted of Me, behold in the contempt of all worldly things and in the avoidance of all worthless pleasures shall be thy blessing, and fulness of consolation shall be given thee. And the more thou withdrawest thyself from all solace of creatures, the more sweet and powerful consolations shalt thou find. But at the first thou shalt not attain to them, without some sorrow and hard striving. Long-accustomed habit will oppose, but it shall be overcome by better habit. The flesh will murmur again and again, but will be restrained by fervour of spirit. The old serpent will urge and embitter thee, but will be put to flight by

prayer; moreover, by useful labour his entrance will be greatly obstructed."

(1) Ecclesiastes xviii. 30.   (2) Psalm xxxvii. 4.

CHAPTER XIII

Of the obedience of one in lowly subjection after the example of Jesus Christ

"My Son, he who striveth to withdraw himself from obedience, withdraweth himself also from grace, and he who seeketh private advantages, loseth those which are common unto all. If a man submit not freely and willingly to one set over him, it is a sign that his flesh is not yet perfectly subject to himself, but often resisteth and murmureth. Learn therefore quickly to submit thyself to him who is over thee, if thou seekest to bring thine own flesh into subjection. For the outward enemy is very quickly overcome if the inner man have not been laid low. There is no more grievous and deadly enemy to the soul than thou art to thyself, if thou art not led by the Spirit. Thou must not altogether conceive contempt for thyself, if thou wilt prevail against flesh and blood. Because as yet thou inordinately lovest thyself, therefore thou shrinkest from yielding thyself to the will of others.

2. "But what great thing is it that thou, who art dust and nothingness, yieldest thyself to man for God's sake, when I, the Almighty and the Most High, who created all things out of nothing, subjected Myself to man for thy sake? I became the most humble and despised of men, that by My humility thou mightest overcome thy pride. Learn to obey, O dust! Learn to humble thyself, O earth and clay, and to bow thyself beneath the feet of all. Learn to crush thy passions, and to yield thyself in all subjection.

3. "Be zealous against thyself, nor suffer pride to live within thee, but so show thyself subject and of no reputation, that all may be able to walk over thee, and tread thee down as the clay in the streets. What hast thou, O foolish man, of which to

complain? What, O vile sinner, canst thou answer those who speak against thee, seeing thou hast so often offended God, and many a time hast deserved hell? But Mine eye hath spared thee, because thy soul was precious in My sight; that thou mightest know My love, and mightest be thankful for My benefits; and that thou mightest give thyself altogether to true subjection and humility, and patiently bear the contempt which thou meritest."

CHAPTER XIV

Of meditation upon the hidden judgments of God, that we may not be lifted up because of our well-doing

Thou sendest forth Thy judgments against me, O Lord, and shakest all my bones with fear and trembling, and my soul trembleth exceedingly. I stand astonished, and remember that the heavens are not clean in thy sight.(1) If Thou chargest Thine angels with folly, and didst spare them not, how shall it be unto me? Stars have fallen from heaven, and what shall I dare who am but dust? They whose works seemed to be praiseworthy, fell into the lowest depths, and they who did eat Angels' food, them have I seen delighted with the husks that the swine do eat.

2. There is therefore no holiness, if Thou O Lord, withdraw Thine hand. No wisdom profiteth, if Thou leave off to guide the helm. No strength availeth, if Thou cease to preserve. No purity is secure, if Thou protect it not. No self-keeping availeth, if Thy holy watching be not there. For when we are left alone we are swallowed up and perish, but when we are visited, we are raised up, and we live. For indeed we are unstable, but are made strong through Thee; we grow cold, but are rekindled by Thee.

3. Oh, how humbly and abjectly must I reckon of myself, how must I weigh it as nothing, if I seem to have nothing good! Oh, how profoundly ought I to submit myself to Thy unfathomable judgments, O Lord, when I find myself nothing else save nothing, and again nothing! Oh weight unmeasurable, oh ocean which cannot be crossed over, where I find nothing of myself save nothing altogether! Where, then, is the hiding-place of glory, where the confidence begotten of virtue? All vain-glory is swallowed up in

the depths of Thy judgments against me.

4. What is all flesh in Thy sight? For how shall the clay boast against Him that fashioned it?(2) How can he be lifted up in vain speech whose heart is subjected in truth to God? The whole world shall not lift him up whom Truth hath subdued; nor shall he be moved by the mouth of all who praise him, who hath placed all his hope in God. For they themselves who speak, behold, they are all nothing; for they shall cease with the sound of their words, but the truth of the Lord endureth for ever.(3)

(1) Job xv. 15.   (2) Psalm xxix. 16.   (3) Psalm cxvii. 2.

CHAPTER XV

How we must stand and speak, in everything that we desire

"My Son, speak thou thus in every matter, 'Lord, if it please Thee, let this come to pass. Lord, if this shall be for Thine honour, let it be done in Thy Name. Lord, if thou see it good for me, and approve it as useful, then grant me to use it for Thy honour. But if thou knowest that it shall be hurtful unto me, and not profitable for the health of my soul, take the desire away from me'! For not every desire is from the Holy Ghost, although it appear to a man right and good. It is difficult to judge with certainty whether a good or an evil spirit move thee to desire this or that, or whether thou art moved by thine own spirit. Many have been deceived at the last, who seemed at the beginning to be moved by a good spirit.

2. "Therefore, whatsoever seemeth to thee desirable, thou must always desire and seek after it with the fear of God and humility of heart, and most of all, must altogether resign thyself, and commit all unto Me and say, 'Lord, thou knowest what is best; let this or that be, according as Thou wilt. Give what Thou wilt, so much as Thou wilt, when Thou wilt. Do with me as Thou knowest best, and as best shall please Thee, and as shall be most to Thine honour. Place me where Thou wilt, and freely work Thy will with me in all things. I am in Thine hand, and turn me in my course. Behold, I am Thy servant, ready for all things; for I

desire to live not to myself but to Thee. Oh, that I might live worthily and perfectly.'"

A PRAYER TO BE ENABLED TO DO GOD'S WILL PERFECTLY

3. Grant me Thy grace, most merciful Jesus, that it may be with me, and work in me, and persevere with me, even unto the end. Grant that I may ever desire and wish whatsoever is most pleasing and dear unto Thee. Let Thy will be mine, and let my will alway follow Thine, and entirely accord with it. May I choose and reject whatsoever Thou dost; yea, let it be impossible for me to choose or reject except according to Thy will.

4. Grant that I may die to all worldly things, and for Thy sake love to be despised and unknown in this world. Grant unto me, above all things that I can desire, to rest in Thee, and that in Thee my heart may be at peace. Thou art the true peace of the heart, Thou alone its rest; apart from Thee all things are hard and unquiet. In Thee alone, the supreme and eternal God, I will lay me down in peace and take my rest.(1) Amen.

(1) Psalm iv. 9.

CHAPTER XVI

That true solace is to be sought in God alone

Whatsoever I am able to desire or to think of for my solace, I look for it not here, but hereafter. For if I alone had all the solaces of this world, and were able to enjoy all its delights, it is certain that they could not endure long. Wherefore, O my soul, thou canst be fully comforted and perfectly refreshed, only in God, the Comforter of the poor, and the lifter up of the humble. Wait but a little while, my soul, wait for the Divine promise, and thou shalt have abundance of all good things in heaven. If thou longest too inordinately for the things which are now, thou shalt lose those which are eternal and heavenly. Let temporal things be in the use, eternal things in the desire. Thou canst not be satisfied with any temporal good, for thou wast not created for the enjoyment of these.

2. Although thou hadst all the good things which ever were created, yet couldst not thou be happy and blessed; all thy blessedness and thy felicity lieth in God who created all things; not such felicity as seemeth good to the foolish lover of the world, but such as Christ's good and faithful servants wait for, and as the spiritual and pure in heart sometimes taste, whose conversation is in heaven.(1) All human solace is empty and short-lived; blessed and true is that solace which is felt inwardly, springing from the truth. The godly man everywhere beareth about with him his own Comforter, Jesus, and saith unto Him: "Be with me, Lord Jesus, always and everywhere. Let it be my comfort to be able to give up cheerfully all human comfort. And if Thy consolation fail me, let Thy will and righteous approval be alway with me for the highest comfort. For Thou wilt not always be chiding, neither keepest Thou Thine anger for ever."(2)

(1) Philippians iii. 20.   (2) Psalm cii. 9.

CHAPTER XVII

That all care is to be cast upon God

"My Son, suffer me to do with thee what I will; I know what is expedient for thee. Thou thinkest as a man, in many things thou judgest as human affection persuadeth thee."

2. Lord, what Thou sayest is true. Greater is Thy care for me than all the care which I am able to take for myself. For too insecurely doth he stand who casteth not all his care upon Thee. Lord, so long as my will standeth right and firm in Thee, do with me what Thou wilt, for whatsoever Thou shalt do with me cannot be aught but good. Blessed be Thou if Thou wilt leave me in darkness: blessed also be Thou if Thou wilt leave me in light. Blessed be Thou if Thou vouchsafe to comfort me, and always blessed be Thou if Thou cause me to be troubled.

3. "My Son! even thus thou must stand if thou desirest to walk

with Me. Thou must be ready alike for suffering or rejoicing. Thou must be poor and needy as willingly as full and rich."

4. Lord, I will willingly bear for Thee whatsoever Thou wilt have to come upon me. Without choice I will receive from Thy hand good and evil, sweet and bitter, joy and sadness, and will give Thee thanks for all things which shall happen unto me. Keep me from all sin, and I will not fear death nor hell. Only cast me not away for ever, nor blot me out of the book of life. Then no tribulation which shall come upon me shall do me hurt.

CHAPTER XVIII

That temporal miseries are to be borne patiently after the example of Christ

"My Son! I came down from heaven for thy salvation; I took upon Me thy miseries not of necessity, but drawn by love that thou mightest learn patience and mightest bear temporal miseries without murmuring. For from the hour of My birth, until My death upon the Cross, I ceased not from bearing of sorrow; I had much lack of temporal things; I oftentimes heard many reproaches against Myself; I gently bore contradictions and hard words; I received ingratitude for benefits, blasphemies for My miracles, rebukes for My doctrine."

2. Lord, because Thou wast patient in Thy life, herein most of all fulfilling the commandment of Thy Father, it is well that I, miserable sinner, should patiently bear myself according to Thy will, and as long as Thou wilt have it so, should bear about with me for my salvation, the burden of this corruptible life. For although the present life seemeth burdensome, it is nevertheless already made very full of merit through Thy grace, and to those who are weak it becometh easier and brighter through Thy example and the footsteps of Thy saints; but it is also much more full of consolation than it was of old, under the old Testament, when the gate of heaven remained shut; and even the way to heaven seemed more obscure when so few cared to seek after the heavenly kingdom. But not even those who were then just and in the way of salvation were able, before Thy Passion and the ransom of Thy

holy Death, to enter the kingdom of heaven.

3. Oh what great thanks am I bound to give Thee, who hast vouchsafed to show me and all faithful people the good and right way to Thine eternal kingdom, for Thy way is our way, and by holy patience we walk to Thee who art our Crown. If Thou hadst not gone before and taught us, who would care to follow? Oh, how far would they have gone backward if they had not beheld Thy glorious example! Behold we are still lukewarm, though we have heard of Thy many signs and discourses; what would become of us if we had not such a light to help us follow Thee?

CHAPTER XIX

Of bearing injuries, and who shall be approved as truly patient

"What sayest thou, My Son? Cease to complain; consider My suffering and that of My saints. Thou hast not yet resisted unto blood.(1) It is little which thou sufferest in comparison with those who have suffered so many things, have been so strongly tempted, so grievously troubled, so manywise proved and tried. Thou oughtest therefore to call to mind the more grievous sufferings of others that thou mightest bear thy lesser ones more easily, and if they seem not to thee little, see that it is not thy impatience which is the cause of this. But whether they be little or whether they be great, study to bear them all with patience.

2. "So far as thou settest thyself to bear patiently, so far thou dost wisely and art deserving of the more merit; thou shalt also bear the more easily if thy mind and habit are carefully trained hereunto. And say not 'I cannot bear these things from such a man, nor are things of this kind to be borne by me, for he hath done me grievous harm and imputeth to me what I had never thought: but from another I will suffer patiently, such things as I see I ought to suffer.' Foolish is such a thought as this, for it considereth not the virtue of patience, nor by whom that virtue is to be crowned, but it rather weigheth persons and offences against self.

3. "He is not truly patient who will only suffer as far as seemeth right to himself and from whom he pleaseth. But the truly patient man considereth not by what man he is tried, whether by one above him, or by an equal or inferior, whether by a good and holy man, or a perverse and unworthy; but indifferently from every creature, whatsoever or how often soever adversity happeneth to him, he gratefully accepteth all from the hand of God and counteth it great gain: for with God nothing which is borne for His sake, however small, shall lose its reward.

4. "Be thou therefore ready for the fight if thou wilt have the victory. Without striving thou canst not win the crown of patience; if thou wilt not suffer thou refusest to be crowned. But if thou desirest to be crowned, strive manfully, endure patiently. Without labour thou drawest not near to rest, nor without fighting comest thou to victory."

5. Make possible to me, O Lord, by grace what seemeth impossible to me by nature. Thou knowest how little I am able to bear, and how quickly I am cast down when a like adversity riseth up against me. Whatsoever trial of tribulation may come to me, may it become unto me pleasing and acceptable, for to suffer and be vexed for Thy sake is exceeding healthful to the soul.

(1) Hebrews xii. 4.

CHAPTER XX

Of confession of our infirmity and of the miseries of this life

I will acknowledge my sin unto Thee;(1) I will confess to Thee, Lord, my infirmity. It is often a small thing which casteth me down and maketh me sad. I resolve that I will act bravely, but when a little temptation cometh, immediately I am in a great strait. Wonderfully small sometimes is the matter whence a grievous temptation cometh, and whilst I imagine myself safe for a little space; when I am not considering, I find myself often almost overcome by a little puff of wind.

2. Behold, therefore, O Lord, my humility and my frailty, which is altogether known to Thee. Be merciful unto me, and draw me out of the mire that I sink not,(2) lest I ever remain cast down. This is what frequently throweth me backward and confoundeth me before Thee, that I am so liable to fall, so weak to resist my passions. And though their assault is not altogether according to my will, it is violent and grievous, and it altogether wearieth me to live thus daily in conflict. Herein is my infirmity made known to me, that hateful fancies always rush in far more easily than they depart.

3. Oh that Thou, most mighty God of Israel, Lover of all faithful souls, wouldst look upon the labour and sorrow of Thy servant, and give him help in all things whereunto he striveth. Strengthen me with heavenly fortitude, lest the old man, this miserable flesh, not being yet fully subdued to the spirit, prevail to rule over me; against which I ought to strive so long as I remain in this most miserable life. Oh what a life is this, where tribulations and miseries cease not, where all things are full of snares and of enemies, for when one tribulation or temptation goeth, another cometh, yea, while the former conflict is yet raging others come more in number and unexpected.

4. And how can the life of man be loved, seeing that it hath so many bitter things, that it is subjected to so many calamities and miseries. How can it be even called life, when it produces so many deaths and plagues? The world is often reproached because it is deceitful and vain, yet notwithstanding it is not easily given up, because the lusts of the flesh have too much rule over it. Some draw us to love, some to hate. The lust of the flesh, the lust of the eyes, and the pride of life, these draw to love of the world; but the punishments and miseries which righteously follow these things, bring forth hatred of the world and weariness.

5. But, alas! an evil desire conquereth a mind given to the world, and thinketh it happiness to be under the nettles(3) because it savoureth not nor perceiveth the sweetness of God nor the inward gracefulness of virtue. But they who perfectly despise the world and strive to live unto God in holy discipline, these are not ignorant of the divine sweetness promised to all

who truly deny themselves and see clearly how grievously the world erreth, and in how many ways it is deceived.

(1) Psalm xxxii. 5.   (2) Psalm lix. 16.   (3) Job xxx. 7.

CHAPTER XXI

That we must rest in God above all goods and gifts

Above all things and in all things thou shalt rest alway in the Lord, O my soul, for he himself is the eternal rest of the saints. Grant me, most sweet and loving Jesus, to rest in Thee above every creature, above all health and beauty, above all glory and honour, above all power and dignity, above all knowledge and skilfulness, above all riches and arts, above all joy and exultation, above all fame and praise, above all sweetness and consolation, above all hope and promise, above all merit and desire, above all gifts and rewards which Thou canst give and pour forth, above all joy and jubilation which the mind is able to receive and feel; in a word, above Angels and Archangels and all the army of heaven, above all things visible and invisible, and above everything which Thou, O my God, art not.

2. For Thou, O Lord, my God, art best above all things; Thou only art the Most High, Thou only the Almighty, Thou only the All-sufficient, and the Fulness of all things; Thou only the All-delightsome and the All-comforting; Thou alone the altogether lovely and altogether loving; Thou alone the Most Exalted and Most Glorious above all things; in Whom all things are, and were, and ever shall be, altogether and all-perfect. And thus it falleth short and is insufficient whatsoever Thou givest to me without Thyself or whatsoever Thou revealest or dost promise concerning Thyself, whilst Thou art not seen or fully possessed: since verily my heart cannot truly rest nor be entirely content, except it rest in Thee, and go beyond all gifts and every creature.

3. O my most beloved Spouse, Jesus Christ, most holy lover of my soul, Ruler of this whole Creation, who shall give me the wings

of true liberty, that I may flee to Thee and find rest? Oh when shall it be given me to be open to receive Thee to the full, and to see how sweet Thou art, O Lord my God? When shall I collect myself altogether in Thee, that because of Thy love I may not feel myself at all, but may know Thee only above every sense and measure, in measure not known to others. But now I ofttimes groan, and bear my sad estate with sorrow; because many evils befall me in this vale of miseries which continually disturb and fill me with sorrow, and encloud me, continually hinder and fill me with care, allure and entangle me, that I cannot have free access to Thee, nor enjoy that sweet intercourse which is always near at hand to the blessed spirits. Let my deep sighing come before Thee, and my manifold desolation on the earth.

4. O Jesus, Light of Eternal Glory, solace of the wandering soul, before Thee my mouth is without speech, and my silence speaketh to Thee. How long will my Lord delay to come unto me? Let Him come unto me, His poor and humble one, and make me glad. Let Him put forth His hand, and deliver His holy one from every snare. Come, Oh come; for without Thee shall be no joyful day or hour, for Thou art my joy, and without Thee is my table empty. I am miserable, and in a manner imprisoned and loaded with fetters, until Thou refresh me by the light of Thy presence, and give me liberty, and show Thy loving countenance.

5. Let others seek some other thing instead of Thee, whatsoever it shall please them; but for my part nothing else pleaseth or shall please, save Thou, my God, my hope, my eternal salvation. I will not hold my peace, nor cease to implore, until Thy grace return, and until Thou speak to me within.

6. "Behold, here I am! Behold, I come to thee, for thou didst call Me. Thy tears and the longing of thy soul, thy humbleness and contrition of heart have inclined Me, and brought Me to thee."

7. And I said Lord, I have called upon Thee, and I have longed to enjoy Thee, being ready to reject everything for Thy sake. For Thou didst first move me to seek Thee. Therefore, blessed be Thou, O Lord, who has wrought this good work upon Thy servant, according to the multitude of Thy mercy. What then hath Thy

servant to say in Thy presence, save to humble himself greatly before Thee, being alway mindful of his own iniquity and vileness. For there is none like unto Thee in all marvels of heaven and earth. Excellent are Thy works, true are Thy judgments, and by Thy Providence are all things governed. Therefore praise and glory be unto Thee, O Wisdom of the Father, let my mouth and my soul and all created things praise and bless Thee together.

CHAPTER XXII

Of the recollection of God's manifold benefits

Open, O Lord, my heart in Thy law, and teach me to walk in the way of Thy commandments. Grant me to understand Thy will and to be mindful of Thy benefits, both general and special, with great reverence and diligent meditation, that thus I may be able worthily to give Thee thanks. Yet I know and confess that I cannot render Thee due praises for the least of Thy mercies. I am less than the least of all the good things which Thou gavest me; and when I consider Thy majesty, my spirit faileth because of the greatness thereof.

2. All things which we have in the soul and in the body, and whatsoever things we possess, whether outwardly or inwardly, naturally or supernaturally, are Thy good gifts, and prove Thee, from whom we have received them all, to be good, gentle, and kind. Although one receiveth many things, and another fewer, yet all are Thine, and without Thee not even the least thing can be possessed. He who hath received greater cannot boast that it is of his own merit, nor lift himself up above others, nor contemn those beneath him; for he is the greater and the better who ascribeth least to himself, and in giving thanks is the humbler and more devout; and he who holdeth himself to be viler than all, and judgeth himself to be the more unworthy, is the apter for receiving greater things.

3. But he who hath received fewer gifts, ought not to be cast down, nor to take it amiss, nor to envy him who is richer; but rather ought he to look unto Thee, and to greatly extol Thy goodness, for Thou pourest forth Thy gifts so richly, so freely

and largely, without respect of persons. All things come of
Thee; therefore in all things shalt thou be praised. Thou
knowest what is best to be given to each; and why this man hath
less, and that more, is not for us but for Thee to understand,
for unto Thee each man's deservings are fully known.

4. Wherefore, O Lord God, I reckon it even a great benefit, not
to have many things, whence praise and glory may appear
outwardly, and after the thought of men. For so it is that he who
considereth his own poverty and vileness, ought not only to draw
therefrom no grief or sorrow, or sadness of spirit, but rather
comfort and cheerfulness; because Thou, Lord, hast chosen the
poor and humble, and those who are poor in this world, to be Thy
friends and acquaintance. So give all Thine apostles witness
whom Thou hast made princes in all lands. Yet they had their
conversation in this world blameless, so humble and meek, without
any malice or deceit, that they even rejoiced to suffer rebukes
for Thy Name's sake,(1) and what things the world hateth, they
embraced with great joy.

5. Therefore ought nothing so much to rejoice him who loveth Thee
and knoweth Thy benefits, as Thy will in him, and the good
pleasure of Thine eternal Providence, wherewith he ought to be so
contented and comforted, that he would as willingly be the least
as any other would be the greatest, as peaceable and contented in
the lowest as in the highest place, and as willingly held of
small and low account and of no name or reputation as to be more
honourable and greater in the world than others. For Thy will
and the love of Thine honour ought to go before all things, and
to please and comfort him more, than all benefits that are given
or may be given to himself.

(1) Acts v. 41.

CHAPTER XXIII

Of four things which bring great peace

"My Son, now will I teach thee the way of peace and of true
liberty."

2. Do, O my Lord, as Thou sayest, for this is pleasing unto me to hear.

3. "Strive, My Son, to do another's will rather than thine own. Choose always to have less rather than more. Seek always after the lowest place, and to be subject to all. Wish always and pray that the will of God be fulfilled in thee. Behold, such a man as this entereth into the inheritance of peace and quietness."

4. O my Lord, this Thy short discourse hath in itself much of perfectness. It is short in words but full of meaning, and abundant in fruit. For if it were possible that I should fully keep it, disturbance would not so easily arise within me. For as often as I feel myself disquieted and weighed down, I find myself to have gone back from this teaching. But Thou, Who art Almighty, and always lovest progress in the soul, vouchsafe more grace, that I may be enabled to fulfil Thy exhortation, and work out my salvation.

A PRAYER AGAINST EVIL THOUGHTS

5. O Lord my God, be not Thou far from me, my God, haste Thee to help me,(1) for many thoughts and great fears have risen up against me, afflicting my soul. How shall I pass through them unhurt? how shall I break through them?

6. "I," saith He, "will go before thee, and make the crooked places straight."(2) I will open the prison doors, and reveal to thee the secret places.

7. Do, Lord, as Thou sayest; and let all evil thoughts fly away before Thy face. This is my hope and my only comfort, to fly unto Thee in all tribulation, to hope in Thee, to call upon Thee from my heart and patiently wait for Thy loving kindness.

A PRAYER FOR ENLIGHTENMENT OF THE MIND

8. Enlighten me, Blessed Jesus, with the brightness of Thy inner light, and cast forth all darkness from the habitation of my heart. Restrain my many wandering thoughts, and carry away the

temptations which strive to do me hurt. Fight Thou mightily for me, and drive forth the evil beasts, so call I alluring lusts, that peace may be within Thy walls and plenteousness of praise within Thy palaces,(3) even in my pure conscience. Command Thou the winds and the storms, say unto the sea, "Be still," say unto the stormy wind, "Hold thy peace," so shall there be a great calm.

9. Oh send forth Thy light and Thy truth,(4) that they may shine upon the earth; for I am but earth without form and void until Thou give me light. Pour forth Thy grace from above; water my heart with the dew of heaven; give the waters of devotion to water the face of the earth, and cause it to bring forth good and perfect fruit. Lift up my mind which is oppressed with the weight of sins, and raise my whole desire to heavenly things; that having tasted the sweetness of the happiness which is from above, it may take no pleasure in thinking of things of earth.

10. Draw me and deliver me from every unstable comfort of creatures, for no created thing is able to satisfy my desire and to give me comfort. Join me to Thyself by the inseparable bond of love, for Thou alone art sufficient to him that loveth Thee, and without Thee all things are vain toys.

(1) Psalm lxxi. 12.   (2) Isaiah xlv. 2.   (3) Psalm cxxii. 7.
(4) Psalm xliii. 3.

CHAPTER XXIV

Of avoiding of curious inquiry into the life of another

"My Son, be not curious, nor trouble thyself with vain cares. What is that to thee? Follow thou Me.(1) For what is it to thee whether a man be this or that, or say or do thus or thus? Thou hast no need to answer for others, but thou must give an answer for thyself. Why therefore dost thou entangle thyself? Behold, I know all men, and I behold all things which are done under the sun; and I know how it standeth with each one, what he thinketh, what he willeth, and to what end his thoughts reach. All things therefore are to be committed to Me; watch thou thyself in godly peace, and leave him who is unquiet to be unquiet as he will. Whatsoever he shall do or say, shall come unto him, for he cannot deceive Me.

2. "Trouble not thyself about the shadow of a great name, nor about the friendship of many, nor about the love of men towards thee. For these things beget distraction and great sorrows of heart. My word should speak freely unto thee, and I would reveal secrets, if only thou didst diligently look for My appearing, and didst open unto Me the gates of thy heart. Be sober and watch unto prayer,(2) and humble thyself in all things."

(1) John xxi. 12.   (2) 1 Peter iv. 7.

CHAPTER XXV

Wherein firm peace of heart and true profit consist

"My Son, I have said, Peace I leave with you, My peace I give unto you, not as the world giveth give I unto you.(1) All men desire peace, but all do not care for the things which belong unto true peace. My peace is with the humble and lowly in heart. Thy peace shall be in much patience. If thou heardest Me, and didst follow My voice, thou shouldest enjoy much peace."

2. What then shall I do, Lord?

3. "In everything take heed to thyself what thou doest, and what thou sayest; and direct all thy purpose to this, that thou please Me alone, and desire or seek nothing apart from Me. But, moreover, judge nothing rashly concerning the words or deeds of others, nor meddle with matters which are not committed to thee; and it may be that thou shalt be disturbed little or rarely. Yet never to feel any disquiet, nor to suffer any pain of heart or body, this belongeth not to the present life, but is the state of eternal rest. Therefore count not thyself to have found true peace, if thou hast felt no grief; nor that then all is well if thou hast no adversary; nor that this is perfect if all things fall out according to thy desire. Nor then reckon thyself to be anything great, or think that thou art specially beloved, if thou

art in a state of great fervour and sweetness of spirit; for not by these things is the true lover of virtue known, nor in them doth the profit and perfection of man consist."

4. In what then, Lord?

5. "In offering thyself with all thy heart to the Divine Will, in not seeking the things which are thine own, whether great or small, whether temporal or eternal; so that thou remain with the same steady countenance in giving of thanks between prosperity and adversity, weighing all things in an equal balance. If thou be so brave and long-suffering in hope that when inward comfort is taken from thee, thou even prepare thy heart for the more endurance, and justify not thyself, as though thou oughtest not to suffer these heavy things, but dost justify Me in all things that I appoint, and dost bless My Holy Name, then dost thou walk in the true and right way of peace, and shalt have a sure hope that thou shalt again behold My face with joy. For if thou come to an utter contempt of thyself, know that then thou shalt enjoy abundance of peace, as much as is possible where thou art but a wayfaring man."

(1) John xiv. 27.

CHAPTER XXVI

Of the exaltation of a free spirit, which humble prayer more deserveth than doth frequent reading

Lord, this is the work of a perfect man, never to slacken his mind from attention to heavenly things, and among many cares to pass along as it were without care, not after the manner of one indifferent, but rather with the privilege of a free mind, cleaving to no creature with inordinate affection.

2. I beseech Thee, my most merciful Lord God, preserve me from the cares of this life, lest I become too much entangled; from many necessities of the body, lest I be taken captive by pleasure; from all obstacles of the spirit, lest I be broken and cast down with cares. I say not from those things which the

vanity of the world goeth about after with all eagerness, but from those miseries, which by the universal curse of mortality weigh down and hold back the soul of thy servant in punishment, that it cannot enter into liberty of spirit, so often as it would.

3. O my God, sweetness unspeakable, turn into bitterness all my fleshly consolation, which draweth me away from the love of eternal things, and wickedly allureth toward itself by setting before me some present delight. Let not, O my God, let not flesh and blood prevail over me, let not the world and its short glory deceive me, let not the devil and his craftiness supplant me. Give me courage to resist, patience to endure, constancy to persevere. Grant, in place of all consolations of the world, the most sweet unction of Thy Spirit, and in place of carnal love, pour into me the love of Thy Name.

4. Behold, food and drink and clothing, and all the other needs appertaining to the support of the body, are burdensome to the devout spirit. Grant that I may use such things with moderation, and that I be not entangled with inordinate affection for them. To cast away all these things is not lawful, because nature must be sustained, but to require superfluities and things which merely minister delight, the holy law forbiddeth; for otherwise the flesh would wax insolent against the spirit. In all these things, I beseech Thee, let Thy hand guide and teach me, that I in no way exceed.

CHAPTER XXVII

That personal love greatly hindereth from the highest good

"My Son, thou must give all for all, and be nothing of thine own. Know thou that the love of thyself is more hurtful to thee than anything in the world. According to the love and inclination which thou hast, everything more or less cleaveth to thee. If thy love be pure, sincere, well-regulated, thou shalt not be in captivity to anything. Do not covet what thou mayest not have; do not have what is able to hinder thee, and to rob thee of inward liberty. It is wonderful that thou committest not thyself

to Me from the very bottom of thy heart, with all things which
thou canst desire or have.

2. "Why art thou consumed with vain sorrow? Why art thou wearied
with superfluous cares? Stand thou by My good pleasure, and thou
shalt suffer no loss. If thou seekest after this or that, and
wilt be here or there, according to thine own advantage or the
fulfilling of thine own pleasure, thou shalt never be in quiet,
nor free from care, because in everything somewhat will be found
lacking, and everywhere there will be somebody who opposeth thee.

3. "Therefore it is not gaining or multiplying of this thing or
that which advantageth thee, but rather the despising it and
cutting it by the root out of thy heart; which thou must not only
understand of money and riches, but of the desire after honour
and vain praise, things which all pass away with the world. The
place availeth little if the spirit of devotion is wanting; nor
shall that peace stand long which is sought from abroad, if the
state of thy heart is without the true foundation, that is, if it
abide not in Me. Thou mayest change, but thou canst not better
thyself; for when occasion ariseth and is accepted thou shalt
find what thou didst fly from, yea more."

A PRAYER FOR CLEANSING OF THE HEART AND FOR HEAVENLY
WISDOM

4. Strengthen me, O God, by the grace of Thy Holy Spirit. Give
me virtue to be strengthened with might in the inner man, and to
free my heart from all fruitless care and trouble, and that I be
not drawn away by various desires after any things whatsoever,
whether of little value or great, but that I may look upon all as
passing away, and myself as passing away with them; because there
is no profit under the sun, and all is vanity and vexation of
spirit.(1) Oh how wise is he that considereth thus!

5. Give me, O Lord, heavenly wisdom, that I may learn to seek
Thee above all things and to find Thee; to relish Thee above all
things and to love Thee; and to understand all other things, even
as they are, according to the order of Thy wisdom. Grant me
prudently to avoid the flatterer, and patiently to bear with him

that opposeth me; for this is great wisdom, not to be carried
by every wind of words, nor to give ear to the wicked flattering
Siren; for thus do we go safely on in the way we have begun.

(1) Ecclesiastes ii. 11.

CHAPTER XXVIII

Against the tongues of detractors

"My Son, take it not sadly to heart, if any think ill of thee,
and say of thee what thou art unwilling to hear. Thou oughtest
to think worse of thyself, and to believe no man weaker than
thyself. If thou walkest inwardly, thou wilt not weigh flying
words above their value. It is no small prudence to keep silence
in an evil time and to turn inwardly unto Me, and not to be
troubled by human judgment.

2. "Let not thy peace depend upon the word of men; for whether
they judge well or ill of thee, thou art not therefore any other
man than thyself. Where is true peace or true glory? Is it not
in Me? And he who seeketh not to please men, nor feareth to
displease, shall enjoy abundant peace. From inordinate love and
vain fear ariseth all disquietude of heart, and all distraction
of the senses."

CHAPTER XXIX

How when tribulation cometh we must call upon and bless God

Blessed be thy name, O Lord, for evermore, who hast willed this
temptation and trouble to come upon me. I cannot escape it, but
have need to flee unto Thee, that Thou mayest succour me and turn
it unto me for good. Lord, now am I in tribulation, and it is
not well within my heart, but I am sore vexed by the suffering
which lieth upon me. And now, O dear Father, what shall I say?
I am taken among the snares. Save me from this hour, but for
this cause came I unto this hour,(1) that Thou mightest be
glorified when I am deeply humbled and am delivered through Thee.

Let it be Thy pleasure to deliver me;(2) for what can I do who am poor, and without Thee whither shall I go? Give patience this time also. Help me, O Lord my God, and I will not fear how much soever I be weighed down.

2. And now amid these things what shall I say? Lord, Thy will be done. I have well deserved to be troubled and weighed down. Therefore I ought to bear, would that it be with patience, until the tempest be overpast and comfort return. Yet is Thine omnipotent arm able also to take this temptation away from me, and to lessen its power that I fall not utterly under it, even as many a time past thou has helped me, O God, my merciful God. And as much as this deliverance is difficult to me, so much is it easy to Thee, O right hand of the most Highest.

(1) John xii. 27.   (2) Psalm xl. 16.

CHAPTER XXX

Of seeking divine help, and the confidence of obtaining grace

"My Son, I the Lord am a stronghold in the day of trouble.(1) Come unto Me, when it is not well with thee.

"This it is which chiefly hindereth heavenly consolation, that thou too slowly betakest thyself unto prayer. For before thou earnestly seekest unto Me, thou dost first seek after many means of comfort, and refresheth thyself in outward things: so it cometh to pass that all things profit thee but little until thou learn that it is I who deliver those who trust in Me; neither beside Me is there any strong help, nor profitable counsel, nor enduring remedy. But now, recovering courage after the tempest, grow thou strong in the light of My mercies, for I am nigh, saith the Lord, that I may restore all things not only as they were at the first, but also abundantly and one upon another.

2. "For is anything too hard for Me, or shall I be like unto one who saith and doeth not? Where is thy faith? Stand fast and with perseverance. Be long-suffering and strong. Consolation will come unto thee in its due season. Wait for Me; yea, wait; I

will come and heal thee. It is temptation which vexeth thee, and a vain fear which terrifieth thee. What doth care about future events bring thee, save sorrow upon sorrow? Sufficient for the day is the evil thereof.(2) It is vain and useless to be disturbed or lifted up about future things which perhaps will never come.

3. "But it is the nature of man to be deceived by fancies of this sort, and it is a sign of a mind which is still weak to be so easily drawn away at the suggestion of the enemy. For he careth not whether he deceive and beguile by true means or false; whether he throw thee down by the love of the present or fear of the future. Therefore let not thy heart be troubled, neither let it be afraid. Believe in Me, and put thy trust in My mercy.(3) When thou thinkest thyself far removed from Me, I am often the nearer. When thou reckonest that almost all is lost, then often is greater opportunity of gain at hand. All is not lost when something goeth contrary to thy wishes. Thou oughtest not to judge according to present feeling, nor so to take or give way to any grief which befalleth thee, as if all hope of escape were taken away.

4. "Think not thyself totally abandoned, although for the time I have sent to thee some tribulation, or have even withdrawn some cherished consolation; for this is the way to the Kingdom of Heaven. And without doubt it is better for thee and for all My other servants, that ye should be proved by adversities, than that ye should have all things as ye would. I know thy hidden thoughts: and that it is very needful for thy soul's health that sometimes thou be left without relish, lest perchance thou be lifted up by prosperity, and desirous to please thyself in that which thou art not. What I have given I am able to take away, and to restore again at My good pleasure.

5. "When I shall have given, it is Mine; when I shall have taken away, I have not taken what is thine; for every good gift and every perfect gift(4) is from me. If I shall have sent upon thee grief or any vexation, be not angry, nor let thy heart be sad; I am able quickly to lift thee up and to change every burden into joy. But I am just and greatly to be praised, when I do thus unto thee.

6. "If thou rightly consider, and look upon it with truth, thou oughtest never to be so sadly cast down because of adversity, but rather shouldst rejoice and give thanks; yea, verily to count it the highest joy that I afflict thee with sorrows and spare thee not. As My Father hath loved Me, so love I you;(5) thus have I spoken unto My beloved disciples: whom I sent forth not unto worldly joys, but to great strivings; not unto honours, but unto contempt; not unto ease, but to labours; not unto rest, but to bring forth much fruit with patience. My son, remember these words."

(1) Nahum i. 7.   (2) Matthew vi. 34.
(3) John xiv. 27; Psalm xiii. 5.   (4) James i. 17.
(5) John xv. 9.

CHAPTER XXXI

Of the neglect of every creature, that the Creator may be found

O Lord, I still need more grace, if I would arrive where neither man nor any other creature may hinder me. For so long as anything keepeth me back, I cannot freely fly unto Thee. He desired eagerly thus to fly, who cried, saying, Oh that I had wings like a dove, for then would I flee away and be at rest. What is more peaceful than the single eye? And what more free than he that desireth nothing upon earth? Therefore must a man rise above every creature, and perfectly forsake himself, and with abstracted mind to stand and behold that Thou, the Creator of all things, hast among Thy creatures nothing like unto Thyself. And except a man be freed from all creatures, he will not be able to reach freely after Divine things. Therefore few are found who give themselves to contemplation, because few know how to separate themselves entirely from perishing and created things.

2. For this much grace is necessary, which may lift up the soul and raise it above itself. And except a man be lifted up in the spirit, and freed from all creatures, and altogether united to God, whatsoever he knoweth, whatsoever even he hath, it mattereth

but little. He who esteemeth anything great save the one only incomprehensible, eternal, good, shall long time be little and lie low. For whatsoever is not God is nothing, and ought to be counted for nothing. Great is the difference between a godly man, illuminated with wisdom, and a scholar learned in knowledge and given to books. Far nobler is that doctrine which floweth down from the divine fulness above, than that which is acquired laboriously by human study.

3. Many are found who desire contemplation, but they do not strive to practice those things which are required thereunto. It is also a great impediment, that much is made of symbols and external signs, and too little of thorough mortification. I know not how it is, and by what spirit we are led, and what we who would be deemed spiritual are aiming at, that we give so great labour and so eager solicitude for transitory and worthless things, and scarcely ever gather our senses together to think at all of our inward condition.

4. Ah, me! Forthwith after a little recollection we rush out of doors, and do not subject our actions to a strict examination. Where our affections are set we take no heed, and we weep not that all things belonging to us are so defiled. For because all flesh had corrupted itself upon the earth, the great deluge came. Since therefore our inmost affections are very corrupt, it followeth of necessity that our actions also are corrupt, being the index of a deficient inward strength. Out of a pure heart proceedeth the fruit of good living.

5. We demand, how much a man hath done; but from how much virtue he acted, is not so narrowly considered. We ask if he be strong, rich, handsome, clever, whether he is a good writer, good singer, good workman; but how poor he may be in spirit, how patient and gentle, how devout and meditative, on these things many are silent. Nature looketh upon the outward appearance of a man, grace turneth its thought to the heart. The former frequently judgeth amiss; the latter trusteth in God, that it may not be deceived.

CHAPTER XXXII

Of self-denial and the casting away all selfishness

"My Son, thou canst not possess perfect liberty unless thou altogether deny thyself. All they are enslaved who are possessors of riches, they who love themselves, the selfish, the curious, the restless; those who ever seek after soft things, and not after the things of Jesus Christ; those who continually plan and devise that which will not stand. For whatsoever cometh not of God shall perish. Hold fast the short and complete saying, 'Renounce all things, and thou shalt find all things; give up thy lust, and thou shalt find rest.' Dwell upon this in thy mind, and when thou art full of it, thou shalt understand all things."

2. O Lord, this is not the work of a day, nor children's play; verily in this short saying is enclosed all the perfection of the religious.

3. "My son, thou oughtest not to be turned aside, nor immediately cast down, because thou hast heard the way of the perfect. Rather oughtest thou to be provoked to higher aims, and at the least to long after the desire thereof. Oh that it were so with thee, and that thou hadst come to this, that thou wert not a lover of thine own self, but wert ready always to My nod, and to his whom I have placed over thee as thy father. Then shouldest thou please Me exceedingly, and all thy life should go on in joy and peace. Thou hast still many things to renounce, which if thou resign not utterly to Me, thou shalt not gain what thou seekest. I counsel thee to buy of Me gold tried in the fire, that thou mayest be rich,(1) that is heavenly wisdom, which despiseth all base things. Put away from thee earthly wisdom, and all pleasure, whether common to men, or thine own.

4. "I tell thee that thou must buy vile things with those which are costly and great in the esteem of men. For wonderfully vile and small, and almost given up to forgetfulness, doth true heavenly wisdom appear, which thinketh not high things of itself, nor seeketh to be magnified upon the earth; many honour it with their lips, but in heart are far from it; it is indeed the precious pearl, which is hidden from many."

(1) Revelation iii. 18.

CHAPTER XXXIII

Of instability of the heart, and of directing the aim towards God

"My Son, trust not thy feeling, for that which is now will be quickly changed into somewhat else. As long as thou livest thou art subject to change, howsoever unwilling; so that thou art found now joyful, now sad; now at peace, now disquieted; now devout, now indevout; now studious, now careless; now sad, now cheerful. But the wise man, and he who is truly learned in spirit, standeth above these changeable things, attentive not to what he may feel in himself, or from what quarter the wind may blow, but that the whole intent of his mind may carry him on to the due and much-desired end. For thus will he be able to remain one and the same and unshaken, the single eye of his desire being steadfastly fixed, through the manifold changes of the world, upon Me.

2. "But according as the eye of intention be the more pure, even so will a man make his way steadfastly through the manifold storms. But in many the eye of pure intention waxeth dim; for it quickly resteth itself upon anything pleasant which occurreth, and rarely is any man found altogether free from the blemish of self-seeking. So the Jews of old came to Bethany, to the house of Martha and Mary, that they might see not Jesus, but Lazarus, whom he had raised from the dead.(1) Therefore must the eye of the intention be cleansed, that it may be single and right, and above all things which come in its way, may be directed unto Me."

(1) John xii. 9.

CHAPTER XXXIV

That to him who loveth God is sweet above all things and in all things

Behold, God is mine, and all things are mine! What will I more, and what more happy thing can I desire? O delightsome and sweet world! that is, to him that loveth the Word, not the world, neither the things that are in the world.(1) My God, my all! To him that understandeth, that word sufficeth, and to repeat it often is pleasing to him that loveth it. When Thou art present all things are pleasant; when Thou art absent, all things are wearisome. Thou makest the heart to be at rest, givest it deep peace and festal joy. Thou makest it to think rightly in every matter, and in every matter to give Thee praise; neither can anything please long without Thee but if it would be pleasant and of sweet savour, Thy grace must be there, and it is Thy wisdom which must give unto it a sweet savour.

2. To him who tasteth Thee, what can be distasteful? And to him who tasteth Thee not, what is there which can make him joyous? But the worldly wise, and they who enjoy the flesh, these fail in Thy wisdom; for in the wisdom of the world is found utter vanity, and to be carnally minded is death. But they who follow after Thee through contempt of worldly things, and mortification of the flesh, are found to be truly wise because they are carried from vanity to verity, from the flesh to the spirit. They taste that the Lord is good, and whatsoever good they find in creatures, they count it all unto the praise of the Creator. Unlike, yea, very unlike is the enjoyment of the Creator to enjoyment of the Creature, the enjoyment of eternity and of time, of light uncreated and of light reflected.

3. O Light everlasting, surpassing all created lights, dart down Thy ray from on high which shall pierce the inmost depths of my heart. Give purity, joy, clearness, life to my spirit that with all its powers it may cleave unto Thee with rapture passing man's understanding. Oh when shall that blessed and longed-for time come when Thou shalt satisfy me with Thy presence, and be unto me All in all? So long as this is delayed, my joy shall not be full. Still, ah me! the old man liveth in me: he is not yet all crucified, not yet quite dead; still he lusteth fiercely against the spirit, wageth inward wars, nor suffereth the soul's kingdom to be in peace.

4. But Thou who rulest the raging of the sea, and stillest the

waves thereof when they arise, rise up and help me. Scatter the people that delight in war.(2) Destroy them by Thy power. Show forth, I beseech Thee, Thy might, and let Thy right hand be glorified, for I have no hope, no refuge, save in Thee, O Lord my God.

(1) 1 John ii. 15.   (2) Psalm lxviii. 30.

CHAPTER XXXV

That there is no security against temptation in this life

"My Son, thou art never secure in this life, but thy spiritual armour will always be needful for thee as long as thou livest. Thou dwellest among foes, and art attacked on the right hand and on the left. If therefore thou use not on all sides the shield of patience, thou wilt not remain long unwounded. Above all, if thou keep not thy heart fixed upon Me with steadfast purpose to bear all things for My sake, thou shalt not be able to bear the fierceness of the attack, nor to attain to the victory of the blessed. Therefore must thou struggle bravely all thy life through, and put forth a strong hand against those things which oppose thee. For to him that overcometh is the hidden manna given,(1) but great misery is reserved for the slothful.

2. "If thou seek rest in this life, how then wilt thou attain unto the rest which is eternal? Set not thyself to attain much rest, but much patience. Seek the true peace, not in earth but in heaven, not in man nor in any created thing, but in God alone. For the love of God thou must willingly undergo all things, whether labours or sorrows, temptations, vexations, anxieties, necessities, infirmities, injuries, gainsayings, rebukes, humiliations, confusions, corrections, despisings; these things help unto virtue, these things prove the scholar of Christ; these things fashion the heavenly crown. I will give thee an eternal reward for short labour, and infinite glory for transient shame.

3. "Thinkest thou that thou shalt always have spiritual consolations at thy will? My Saints had never such, but instead thereof manifold griefs, and divers temptations, and heavy

desolations. But patiently they bore themselves in all, and
trusted in God more than in themselves, knowing that the
sufferings of this present time are not worthy to be compared
with the glory which shall be revealed in us.(2) Wouldst thou
have that immediately which many have hardly attained unto after
many tears and hard labours? Wait for the Lord, quit thyself
like a man and be strong; be not faint-hearted, nor go aside from
Me, but constantly devote thy body and soul to the glory of God.
I will reward thee plenteously, I will be with thee in
trouble."(3)

(1) Revelation ii. 17.   (2) Romans viii. 17.
(3) Psalm xci. 15.

CHAPTER XXXVI

Against vain judgments of men

"My Son, anchor thy soul firmly upon God, and fear not man's
judgment, when conscience pronounceth thee pious and innocent.
It is good and blessed thus to suffer; nor will it be grievous to
the heart which is humble, and which trusteth in God more than in
itself. Many men have many opinions, and therefore little trust
is to be placed in them. But moreover it is impossible to please
all. Although Paul studied to please all men in the Lord, and to
become all things to all men,(1) yet nevertheless with him it was
a very small thing that he should be judged by man's
judgment."(2)

2. He laboured abundantly, as much as in him lay, for the
building up and the salvation of others; but he could not avoid
being sometimes judged and despised by others. Therefore he
committed all to God, who knew all, and by patience and humility
defended himself against evil speakers, or foolish and false
thinkers, and those who accused him according to their pleasure.
Nevertheless, from time to time he replied, lest his silence
should become a stumbling-block to those who were weak.

3. "Who art thou, that thou shouldst be afraid of a man that
shall die? To-day he is, and to-morrow his place is not found.

Fear God and thou shalt not quail before the terrors of men.
What can any man do against thee by words or deeds? He hurteth
himself more than thee, nor shall he escape the judgment of God,
whosoever he may be. Have thou God before thine eyes, and do not
contend with fretful words. And if for the present thou seem to
give way, and to suffer confusion which thou hast not deserved,
be not angry at this, nor by impatience diminish thy reward; but
rather look up to Me in heaven, for I am able to deliver thee
from all confusion and hurt, and to render to every man according
to his works."

(1) 1 Corinthians ix. 22.   (2) 1 Corinthians iv. 3.

CHAPTER XXXVII

Of pure and entire resignation of self, for the obtaining
liberty of heart

"My Son, lose thyself and thou shalt find Me. Stand still
without all choosing and all thought of self, and thou shalt ever
be a gainer. For more grace shall be added to thee, as soon as
thou resignest thyself, and so long as thou dost not turn back to
take thyself again."

2. O Lord, how often shall I resign myself, and in what things
shall I lose myself?

3. "Always; every hour: in that which is little, and in that
which is great. I make no exception, but will that thou be found
naked in all things. Otherwise how canst thou be Mine and I
thine, unless thou be inwardly and outwardly free from every will
of thine own? The sooner thou dost this, the better shall it be
with thee; and the more fully and sincerely, the more thou shalt
please Me, and the more abundantly shalt thou be rewarded.

4. "Some resign themselves, but with certain reservations, for
they do not fully trust in God, therefore they think that they
have some provision to make for themselves. Some again at first
offer everything; but afterwards being pressed by temptation they
return to their own devices, and thus make no progress in virtue.

They will not attain to the true liberty of a pure heart, nor to the grace of My sweet companionship, unless they first entirely resign themselves and daily offer themselves up as a sacrifice; without this the union which bringeth forth fruit standeth not nor will stand.

5. "Many a time I have said unto thee, and now say again, Give thyself up, resign thyself, and thou shalt have great inward peace. Give all for all; demand nothing, ask nothing in return; stand simply and with no hesitation in Me, and thou shalt possess Me. Thou shalt have liberty of heart, and the darkness shall not overwhelm thee. For this strive thou, pray for it, long after it, that thou mayest be delivered from all possession of thyself, and nakedly follow Jesus who was made naked for thee; mayest die unto thyself and live eternally to Me. Then shall all vain fancies disappear, all evil disturbings, and superfluous cares. Then also shall immoderate fear depart from thee, and inordinate love shall die."

CHAPTER XXXVIII

Of a good government in external things, and of having recourse to God in dangers

"My Son, for this thou must diligently make thy endeavour, that in every place and outward action or occupation thou mayest be free within, and have power over thyself; and that all things be under thee, not thou under them; that thou be master and ruler of thy actions, not a slave or hireling, but rather a free and true Hebrew, entering into the lot and the liberty of the children of God, who stand above the present and look upon the eternal, who with the left eye behold things transitory, and with the right things heavenly; whom temporal things draw not to cleave unto, but who rather draw temporal things to do them good service, even as they were ordained of God to do, and appointed by the Master Workman, who hath left nought in His creation without aim and end.

2. "And if in any chance of life thou stand not in outward appearances, nor judgest things which are seen and heard by the

fleshly sense, but straightway in every cause enterest with Moses into the tabernacle to ask counsel of God; thou shalt hear a divine response and come forth instructed concerning many things that are and shall be. For always Moses had recourse to the tabernacle for the solving of all doubts and questionings; and fled to the help of prayer to be delivered from the dangers and evil deeds of men. Thus also oughtest thou to fly to the secret chamber of thy heart, and earnestly implore the divine succour. For this cause we read that Joshua and the children of Israel were deceived by the Gibeonites, that they asked not counsel at the mouth of the Lord,(1) but being too ready to listen to fair speeches, were deceived by pretended piety."

(1) Joshua ix. 14.

CHAPTER XXXIX

That man must not be immersed in business

"My Son, always commit thy cause to Me; I will dispose it aright in due time. Wait for My arrangement of it, and then thou shalt find it for thy profit."

2. O Lord, right freely I commit all things to Thee; for my planning can profit but little. Oh that I did not dwell so much on future events, but could offer myself altogether to Thy pleasures without delay.

3. "My Son, a man often striveth vehemently after somewhat which he desireth; but when he hath obtained it he beginneth to be of another mind, because his affections towards it are not lasting, but rather rush on from one thing to another. Therefore it is not really a small thing, when in small things we resist self."

4. The true progress of man lieth in self-denial, and a man who denieth himself is free and safe. But the old enemy, opposer of all good things, ceaseth not from temptation; but day and night setteth his wicked snares, if haply he may be able to entrap the unwary. Watch and pray, saith the Lord, lest ye enter into temptation.(1)

(1) Matthew xxvi. 41.

CHAPTER XL

That man hath no good in himself, and nothing whereof to glory

Lord, what is man that Thou art mindful of him, or the son of man that Thou visitest him?(1) What hath man deserved, that Thou shouldest bestow thy favour upon him? Lord, what cause can I have of complaint, if Thou forsake me? Or what can I justly allege, if Thou refuse to hear my petition? Of a truth, this I may truly think and say, Lord, I am nothing, I have nothing that is good of myself, but I fall short in all things, and ever tend unto nothing. And unless I am helped by Thee and inwardly supported, I become altogether lukewarm and reckless.

2. But Thou, O Lord, art always the same, and endurest for ever, always good, righteous, and holy; doing all things well, righteously, and holily, and disposing all in Thy wisdom. But I who am more ready to go forward than backward, never continue in one stay, because changes sevenfold pass over me. Yet it quickly becometh better when it so pleaseth Thee, and Thou puttest forth Thy hand to help me; because Thou alone canst aid without help of man, and canst so strengthen me that my countenance shall be no more changed, but my heart shall be turned to Thee, and rest in Thee alone.

3. Wherefore, if I but knew well how to reject all human consolations, whether for the sake of gaining devotion, or because of the necessity by which I was compelled to seek Thee, seeing there is no man who can comfort me; then could I worthily trust in Thy grace, and rejoice in the gift of new consolation.

4. Thanks be to Thee, from whom all cometh, whensoever it goeth well with me! But I am vanity and nothing in Thy sight, a man inconstant and weak. What then have I whereof to glory, or why do I long to be held in honour? Is it not for nought? This also is utterly vain. Verily vain glory is an evil plague, the greatest of vanities, because it draweth us away from the true

glory, and robbeth us of heavenly grace. For whilst a man pleaseth himself he displeaseth Thee; whilst he gapeth after the praises of man, he is deprived of true virtues.

5. But true glory and holy rejoicing lieth in glorying in Thee and not in self; in rejoicing in Thy Name, not in our own virtue; in not taking delight in any creature, save only for Thy sake. Let thy Name, not mine be praised; let Thy work, not mine be magnified; let Thy holy Name be blessed, but to me let nought be given of the praises of men. Thou art my glory, Thou art the joy of my heart. In Thee will I make my boast and be glad all the day long, but for myself let me not glory save only in my infirmities.(2)

6. Let the Jews seek the honour which cometh from one another; but I will ask for that which cometh from God only.(3) Truly all human glory, all temporal honour, all worldly exultation, compared to Thy eternal glory, is but vanity and folly. O God my Truth and my Mercy, Blessed Trinity, to Thee alone be all praise, honour, power, and glory for ever and for ever. Amen.

(1) Psalm viii. 4.   (2) 2 Corinthians xii. 5.
(3) John v. 44.

CHAPTER XLI

Of contempt of all temporal honour

"My Son, make it no matter of thine, if thou see others honoured and exalted, and thyself despised and humbled. Lift up thine heart to Me in heaven, and then the contempt of men upon earth will not make thee sad."

2. O Lord, we are in blindness, and are quickly seduced by vanity. If I look rightly within myself, never was injury done unto me by any creature, and therefore I have nought whereof to complain before Thee. But because I have many times and grievously sinned against Thee, all creatures do justly take arms against me. Therefore to me confusion and contempt are justly due, but to Thee praise and honour and glory. And except I

dispose myself for this, namely, to be willing that every creature should despise and desert me, and that I should be esteemed altogether as nothing, I cannot be inwardly filled with peace and strength, nor spiritually enlightened, nor fully united to Thee.

CHAPTER XLII

That our peace is not to be placed in men

"My Son, if thou set thy peace on any person because thou hast high opinion of him, and art familiar with him, thou shalt be unstable and entangled. But if thou betake thyself to the ever-living and abiding Truth, the desertion or death of a friend shall not make thee sad. In Me ought the love of thy friend to subsist, and for My sake is every one to be loved, whosoever he be, who appeareth to thee good, and is very dear to thee in this life. Without Me friendship hath no strength or endurance, neither is that love true and pure, which I unite not. Thou oughtest to be so dead to such affections of beloved friends, that as far as in thee lieth, thou wouldst rather choose to be without any companionship of men. The nearer a man approacheth to God, the further he recedeth from all earthly solace. The deeper also he descendeth into himself, and the viler he appeareth in his own eyes, the higher he ascendeth towards God.

2. "But he who attributeth anything good to himself, hindereth the grace of God from coming to him, because the grace of the Holy Ghost ever seeketh the humble heart. If thou couldst make thyself utterly nothing, and empty thyself of the love of every creature, then should it be My part to overflow unto thee with great grace. When thou settest thine eyes upon creatures, the face of the Creator is withdrawn from thee. Learn in all things to conquer thyself for thy Creator's sake, then shalt thou be able to attain unto divine knowledge. How small soever anything be, if it be loved and regarded inordinately, it holdeth us back from the highest good, and corrupteth."

CHAPTER XLIII

Against vain and worldly knowledge

"My Son, let not the fair and subtle sayings of men move thee. For the kingdom of God is not in word, but in power.(1) Give ear to My words, for they kindle the heart and enlighten the mind, they bring contrition, and they supply manifold consolations. Never read thou the word that thou mayest appear more learned or wise; but study for the mortification of thy sins, for this will be far more profitable for thee than the knowledge of many difficult questions.

2. "When thou hast read and learned many things, thou must always return to one first principle. I am He that teacheth man knowledge,(2) and I give unto babes clearer knowledge than can be taught by man. He to whom I speak will be quickly wise and shall grow much in the spirit. Woe unto them who inquire into many curious questions from men, and take little heed concerning the way of My service. The time will come when Christ will appear, the Master of masters, the Lord of the Angels, to hear the lessons of all, that is to examine the consciences of each one. And then will He search Jerusalem with candles,(3) and the hidden things of darkness(4) shall be made manifest, and the arguings of tongues shall be silent.

3. "I am He who in an instant lift up the humble spirit, to learn more reasonings of the Eternal Truth, than if a man had studied ten years in the schools. I teach without noise of words, without confusion of opinions, without striving after honour, without clash of arguments. I am He who teach men to despise earthly things, to loathe things present, to seek things heavenly, to enjoy things eternal, to flee honours, to endure offences, to place all hope in Me, to desire nothing apart from Me, and above all things to love Me ardently.

4. "For there was one, who by loving Me from the bottom of his heart, learned divine things, and spake things that were wonderful; he profited more by forsaking all things than by studying subtleties. But to some I speak common things, to others special; to some I appear gently in signs and figures, and

again to some I reveal mysteries in much light. The voice of
books is one, but it informeth not all alike; because I inwardly
am the Teacher of truth, the Searcher of the heart, the Discerner
of the thoughts, the Mover of actions, distributing to each man,
as I judge meet."

(1) 1 Corinthians iv. 20.   (2) Psalm xciv. 10.
(3) Zephaniah i. 12.   (4) 1 Corinthians iv. 5.

CHAPTER XLIV

Of not troubling ourselves about outward things

"My Son, in many things it behoveth thee to be ignorant, and to
esteem thyself as one dead upon the earth, and as one to whom the
whole world is crucified. Many things also thou must pass by
with deaf ear, and must rather think upon those things which
belong unto thy peace. It is more profitable to turn away thine
eyes from those things that displease, and to leave each man to
his own opinion, than to give thyself to discourses of strife.
If thou stand well with God and hast His judgment in thy mind,
thou wilt verily easily bear to be as one conquered."

2. O Lord, to what have we come? Behold a temporal loss is
mourned over; for a trifling gain we labour and hurry; and
spiritual loss passeth away into forgetfulness, and we rarely
recover it. That which profiteth little or nothing is looked
after, and that which is altogether necessary is negligently
passed by; because the whole man slideth away to outward things,
and unless he quickly recovereth himself in outward things he
willingly lieth down.

CHAPTER XLV

That we must not believe everyone, and that we are prone to fall
in our words

Lord, be thou my help in trouble, for vain is the help of man.(1)
How often have I failed to find faithfulness, where I thought I

possessed it. How many times I have found it where I least
expected. Vain therefore is hope in men, but the salvation of
the just, O God, is in Thee. Blessed be thou, O Lord my God, in
all things which happen unto us. We are weak and unstable, we
are quickly deceived and quite changed.

2. Who is the man who is able to keep himself so warily and
circumspectly as not sometimes to come into some snare of
perplexity? But he who trusteth in Thee, O Lord, and seeketh
Thee with an unfeigned heart, doth not so easily slip. And if he
fall into any tribulation, howsoever he may be entangled, yet
very quickly he shall be delivered through Thee, or by Thee shall
be comforted, because Thou wilt not forsake him that trusteth in
Thee unto the end. A friend who continueth faithful in all the
distresses of his friend is rare to be found. Thou, O Lord, Thou
alone art most faithful in all things, and there is none other
like unto Thee.

3. Oh, how truly wise was that holy soul which said, "My mind is
steadfastly fixed, and it is grounded in Christ."(2) If thus it
were with me, the fear of man should not so easily tempt me, nor
the arrows of words move me. Who is sufficient to foresee all
things, who to guard beforehand against future ills? If even
things which are foreseen sometimes hurt us, what can things
which are not foreseen do, but grievously injure? But wherefore
have I not better provided for myself, miserable that I am? Why,
too, have I given such heed to others? But we are men, nor are
we other than frail men, even though by many we are reckoned and
called angels. Whom shall I trust, O Lord, whom shall I trust
but Thee? Thou art the Truth, and deceivest not, nor canst be
deceived. And on the other hand, Every man is a liar,(3) weak,
unstable and frail, especially in his words, so that one ought
scarcely ever to believe what seemeth to sound right on the face
of it.

4. With what wisdom hast thou warned us beforehand to beware of
men, and that a man's foes are they of his own household,(4) and
that we must not believe if one say unto us Lo here, or Lo
there.(5) I have been taught by my loss, and O that I may prove
more careful and not foolish hereby. "Be cautious," saith some
one: "be cautious, keep unto thyself what I tell thee." And

whilst I am silent and believe that it is hid with me, he himself cannot keep silence concerning it, but straightway betrayeth me and himself, and goeth his way. Protect me, O Lord, from such mischief-making and reckless men; let me not fall into their hands, nor ever do such things myself. Put a true and steadfast word into my mouth, and remove a deceitful tongue far from me. What I would not suffer, I ought by all means to beware of doing.

5. Oh, how good and peacemaking a thing it is to be silent concerning others, and not carelessly to believe all reports, nor to hand them on further; how good also to lay one's self open to few, to seek ever to have Thee as the beholder of the heart; not to be carried about with every wind of words, but to desire that all things inward and outward be done according to the good pleasure of Thy will! How safe for the preserving of heavenly grace to fly from human approval, and not to long after the things which seem to win admiration abroad, but to follow with all earnestness those things which bring amendment of life and heavenly fervour! How many have been injured by their virtue being made known and too hastily praised. How truly profitable hath been grace preserved in silence in this frail life, which, as we are told, is all temptation and warfare.

(1) Psalm lx. 11.   (2) St. Agatha.
(3) Psalm cxvi. 11; Romans iii. 4.   (4) Matthew x. 17, 36.
(5) Matthew xxiv. 23.

CHAPTER XLVI

Of having confidence in God when evil words are cast at us

"My Son, stand fast and believe in Me. For what are words but words? They fly through the air, but they bruise no stone. If thou are guilty, think how thou wouldst gladly amend thyself; if thou knowest nothing against thyself, consider that thou wilt gladly bear this for God's sake. It is little enough that thou sometimes hast to bear hard words, for thou art not yet able to bear hard blows. And wherefore do such trivial matters go to thine heart, except that thou art yet carnal, and regardest men more than thou oughtest? For because thou fearest to be despised, thou art unwilling to be reproved for thy faults, and seekest paltry shelters of excuses.

2. "But look better into thyself, and thou shalt know that the world is still alive in thee, and the vain love of pleasing men. For when thou fleest away from being abased and confounded for thy faults, it is plain that thou art neither truly humble nor truly dead to the world, and that the world is not crucified to thee. But hearken to My word, and thou shalt not care for ten thousand words of men. Behold, if all things could be said against thee which the utmost malice could invent, what should it hurt thee if thou wert altogether to let it go, and make no more account of it than of a mote? Could it pluck out a single hair of thy head?

3. "But he that hath no heart within him, and hath not God before his eyes, is easily moved by a word of reproach; but he who trusteth in Me, and seeketh not to abide by his own judgment, shall be free from the fear of men. For I am the Judge and the Discerner of all secrets; I know how the thing hath been done; I know both the injurer and the bearer. From Me went forth that word, by My permission this hath happened, that the thoughts of many hearts may be revealed.(1) I shall judge the guilty and the innocent; but beforehand I have willed to try them both by a secret judgment.

4. "The testimony of men often deceiveth. My judgment is true; it will stand, and it shall not be overturned. It commonly lieth hid, and only to few in certain cases is it made known; yet it never erreth, nor can err, although it seem not right to the eyes of foolish men. To Me, therefore, must men have recourse in all judgment, and must not lean to their opinion. For there shall no evil happen to the just,(2) whatsoever may be sent to him by God. Even though some unjust charge be brought against him, he will care little; nor, again, will he exult above measure, if through others he be clearly vindicated. For he considereth that I am He who try the hearts and reins,(3) who judge not outwardly and according to human appearance; for often in Mine eyes that is found blameworthy which in the judgment of men is held worthy of praise."

5. O Lord God, O Judge, just, strong, and patient, who knowest the frailty and sinfulness of men, be Thou my strength and my whole confidence; for my own conscience sufficeth me not. Thou knowest what I know not; and therefore ought I under all rebuke to humble myself, and to bear it meekly. Therefore mercifully forgive me as often as I have not done this, and grant me the next time the grace of greater endurance. For better unto me is Thine abundant pity for the attainment of Thy pardon, than the righteousness which I believe myself to have for defence against my conscience, which lieth wait against me. Although I know nothing against myself, yet I am not hereby justified,(4) because if Thy mercy were removed away, in Thy sight should no man living be justified.(5)

(1) Luke ii. 35.   (2) Proverbs xii. 21.   (3) Psalm vii. 9.
(4) 1 Corinthians iv. 4.   (5) Psalm cxliii. 2.

CHAPTER XLVII

That all troubles are to be endured for the sake of eternal life

"My Son, let not the labours which thou hast undertaken for Me break thee down, nor let tribulations cast thee down in any wise, but let my promise strengthen and comfort thee in every event. I am sufficient to reward thee above all measure and extent. Not long shalt thou labour here, nor always be weighed down with sorrows. Wait yet a little while, and thou shalt see a speedy end of thine evils. An hour shall come when all labour and confusion shall cease. Little and short is all that passeth away with time.

2. "Do earnestly what thou dost; labour faithfully in My vineyard; I will be thy reward. Write, read, sing, weep, be silent, pray, endure adversities manfully; eternal life is worthy of all these conflicts, yea, and of greater. Peace shall come in one day which is known to the Lord; which shall be neither day nor night,(1) but light eternal, infinite clearness, steadfast peace, and undisturbed rest. Thou shalt not say then, Who shall deliver me from the body of this death?(2) nor cry out, Woe is me, for my sojourning is prolonged,(3) because death will be

utterly destroyed, and there shall be salvation which can never fail, no more anxiety, happy delight, sweet and noble society.

3. "Oh, if thou sawest the unfading crowns of the Saints in heaven, and with what great glory they now rejoice, who aforetime were reckoned by this world contemptibly and as it were unworthy of life, truly thou wouldst immediately humble thyself even to the earth, and wouldst desire rather to be in subjection to all, than to have authority over one; nor wouldst thou long for pleasant days of this life, but wouldst more rejoice to be afflicted for God's sake, and wouldst esteem it gain to be counted for nought amongst men.

4. "Oh, if these things were sweet to thy taste, and moved thee to the bottom of thine heart, how shouldst thou dare even once to complain? Are not all laborious things to be endured for the sake of eternal life? It is no small thing, the losing or gaining the Kingdom of God. Lift up therefore thy face to heaven. Behold, I and all My Saints with Me, who in this world had a hard conflict, now rejoice, are now comforted, are now secure, are now at peace, and shall remain with Me evermore in the Kingdom of My Father."

(1) Zechariah xiv. 7.   (2) Romans vii. 24. (3) Psalm cxx.

CHAPTER XLVIII

Of the day of eternity and of the straitnesses of this life

Oh most blessed mansion of the City which is above! Oh most clear day of eternity which the night obscureth not, but the Supreme Truth ever enlighteneth! Day always joyful, always secure and never changing its state into those which are contrary. Oh would that this day might shine forth, and that all these temporal things would come to an end. It shineth indeed upon the Saints, glowing with unending brightness, but only from afar and through a glass, upon those who are pilgrims on the earth.

2. The citizens of heaven know how glorious that day is; the

exiled sons of Eve groan, because this is bitter and wearisome. The days of this life are few and evil, full of sorrows and straits, where man is defiled with many sins, ensnared with many passions, bound fast with many fears, wearied with many cares, distracted with many questionings, entangled with many vanities, compassed about with many errors, worn away with many labours, weighed down with temptations, enervated by pleasures, tormented by poverty.

3. Oh when shall there be an end of these evils? When shall I be delivered from the wretched slavery of my sins? When shall I be mindful, O Lord, of Thee alone? When shall I rejoice in Thee to the full? When shall I be in true liberty without any impediment, without any burden on mind or body? When shall there be solid peace, peace immovable and secure, peace within and without, peace firm on every side? Blessed Jesus, when shall I stand to behold Thee? When shall I gaze upon the glory of Thy kingdom? When shalt Thou be to me all in all? Oh when shall I be with Thee in Thy Kingdom which Thou hast prepared from the foundation of the world for them that love Thee? I am left destitute, an exile in a hostile land, where are daily wars and grievous misfortunes.

4. Console my exile, mitigate my sorrow, for towards Thee all my desire longeth. For all is to me a burden, whatsoever this world offereth for consolation. I yearn to enjoy Thee intimately, but I cannot attain unto it. I long to cleave to heavenly things, but temporal things and unmortified passions press me down. In my mind I would be above all things, but in my flesh I am unwillingly compelled to be beneath them. So, wretched man that I am, I fight with myself, and am made grievous even unto myself, while the spirit seeketh to be above and the flesh to be beneath.

5. Oh how I suffer inwardly, while with the mind I discourse on heavenly things, and presently a crowd of carnal things rusheth upon me whilst I pray. My God, be not Thou far from me, nor depart in wrath from Thy servant. Cast forth Thy lightning and scatter them; send out Thine arrows,(1) and let all delusions of my enemy be confounded. Recall my senses unto Thyself, cause me to forget all worldly things; grant me quickly to cast away and despise the imaginations of sin. Succour me, O Eternal Truth,

that no vanity may move me. Come unto me, O Heavenly Sweetness, and let all impurity flee from before Thy face. Pardon me also, and of Thy mercy deal gently with me, whensoever in prayer I think on anything besides Thee; for truly I confess that I am wont to be continually distracted. For often and often, where in the body I stand or sit, there I myself am not; but rather am I there, whither I am borne by my thoughts. Where my thought is, there am I; and there commonly is my thought where that which I love is. That readily occurreth to me, which naturally delighteth, or pleaseth through custom.

6. Wherefore Thou, who art the Truth, hast plainly said, Where your treasure is, there will your heart be also.(2) If I love heaven, I gladly meditate on heavenly things. If I love the world, I rejoice in the delights of the world, and am made sorry by its adversities. If I love the flesh, I am continually imagining the things which belong to the flesh; if I love the spirit, I am delighted by meditating on spiritual things. For whatsoever things I love, on these I readily converse and listen, and carry home with me the images of them. But blessed is that man who for Thy sake, O Lord, is willing to part from all creatures; who doth violence to his fleshly nature and crucifieth the lusts of the flesh by the fervour of his spirit, so that with serene conscience he may offer unto Thee a pure prayer, and be made worthy to enter into the angelic choirs, having shut out from himself, both outwardly and inwardly, all worldly things.

(1) Psalm lxxi. 12.   (2) Matthew vi. 21.

CHAPTER XLIX

Of the desire after eternal life, and how great blessings are promised to those who strive

"My Son, when thou feelest the desire of eternal happiness to be poured into thee from above, and longest to depart from the tabernacle of this body, that thou mayest contemplate My glory without shadow of turning, enlarge thine heart, and take in this holy inspiration with all thy desire. Give most hearty thanks to the Supreme Goodness, who dealeth with thee so graciously, visiteth thee so lovingly, stirreth thee up so fervently, raiseth thee so powerfully, lest thou sink down through thine own weight, to earthly things. For not by thine own meditating or striving dost thou receive this gift, but by the sole gracious condescension of Supreme Grace and Divine regard; to the end that thou mayest make progress in virtue and in more humility, and prepare thyself for future conflicts, and cleave unto Me with all the affection of thy heart, and strive to serve Me with fervent will.

2. "My Son, often the fire burneth, but the flame ascendeth not without smoke. So also the desires of some men burn towards heavenly things, and yet they are not free from the temptation of carnal affection. Thus therefore they are not acting with an altogether simple desire for God's glory when they pray to Him so earnestly. Such, too, is oftentimes thy desire, when thou hast imagined it to be so earnest. For that is not pure and perfect which is tainted with thine own self-seeking.

3. "Seek thou not what is pleasant and advantageous to thyself, but what is acceptable and honourable unto Me; for if thou judgest rightly, thou must choose and follow after My appointment rather than thine own desire; yea, rather than anything that can be desired. I know thy desire, and I have heard thy many groanings. Already thou longest to be in the glorious liberty of the children of God; already the eternal home delighteth thee, and the heavenly country full of joy; but the hour is not yet come; there remaineth still another season, even a season of warfare, a season of labour and probation. Thou desirest to be filled with the Chief Good, but thou canst not attain it immediately. I AM that Good; wait for Me, until the Kingdom of God shall come.

4. "Thou must still be tried upon earth, and be exercised in many things. Consolation shall from time to time be given thee, but abundant satisfying shall not be granted. Be strong therefore, and be thou brave both in working and in suffering things which are against thy nature. Thou must put on the new man, and be changed into another man. Thou must often do what thou wouldst not; and thou must leave undone what thou wouldst do. What pleaseth others shall have good success, what pleaseth thee shall

have no prosperity. What others say shall be listened to; what
thou sayest shall receive no heed. Others shall ask and receive;
thou shalt ask and not obtain. Others shall be great in the
report of men, but about thee shall nothing be spoken. To others
this or that shall be entrusted; thou shalt be judged useful for
nought.

5. "For this cause nature shall sometimes be filled with sadness;
and it is a great thing if thou bear it silently. In this and
many like things the faithful servant of the Lord is wont to be
tried, how far he is able to deny himself and bring himself into
subjection in all things. Scarcely is there anything in which
thou hast need to mortify thyself so much as in seeing things
which are adverse to thy will; especially when things are
commanded thee to be done which seem to thee inexpedient or of
little use to thee. And because thou darest not resist a higher
power, being under authority, therefore it seemeth hard for thee
to shape thy course according to the nod of another, and to
forego thine own opinion.

6. "But consider, My Son, the fruit of these labours, the swift
end, and the reward exceeding great; and thou shalt find it no
pain to bear them then, but rather the strongest solace of thy
patience. For even in exchange for this trifling desire which
thou hast readily forsaken, thou shalt always have thy will in
Heaven. There verily thou shalt find all that thou wouldst, all
that thou canst long for. There thou shalt have all good within
thy power without the fear of losing it. There thy will, ever at
one with Mine, shall desire nothing outward, nothing for itself.
There no man shall withstand thee, none shall complain of thee,
none shall hinder, nothing shall stand in thy path; but all
things desired by thee shall be present together, and shall
refresh thy whole affection, and fill it up even to the brim.
There I will glory for the scorn suffered here, the garment of
praise for sorrow, and for the lowest place a throne in the
Kingdom, for ever. There shall appear the fruit of obedience,
the labour of repentance shall rejoice, and humble subjection
shall be crowned gloriously.

7. "Now therefore bow thyself humbly under the hands of all men;
nor let it trouble thee who said this or who ordered that; but

take special heed that whether thy superior, thy inferior, or thy equal, require anything from thee, or even show a desire for it; take it all in good part, and study with a good will to fulfil the desire. Let one seek this, another that; let this man glory in this, and that man in that, and be praised a thousand thousand times, but rejoice thou only in the contempt of thyself, and in Mine own good pleasure and glory. This is what thou art to long for, even that whether by life or by death God may be ever magnified in thee."[1]

[1] Philippians i. 20.

CHAPTER L

How a desolate man ought to commit himself into the hands of God

O Lord, Holy Father, be Thou blessed now and evermore; because as Thou wilt so it is done, and what Thou doest is good. Let Thy servant rejoice in Thee, not in himself, nor in any other; because Thou alone art the true joy, Thou art my hope and my crown, Thou art my joy and my honour, O Lord. What hath Thy servant, which he received not from Thee, even without merit of his own? Thine are all things which Thou hast given, and which Thou hast made. I am poor and in misery even from my youth up,[1] and my soul is sorrowful unto tears, sometimes also it is disquieted within itself, because of the sufferings which are coming upon it.

2. I long after the joy of peace; for the peace of Thy children do I beseech, for in the light of Thy comfort they are fed by Thee. If Thou give peace, if Thou pour into me holy joy, the soul of Thy servant shall be full of melody, and devout in Thy praise. But if Thou withdraw Thyself as too often Thou art wont, he will not be able to run in the way of Thy commandments, but rather he will smite his breast and will bow his knees; because it is not with him as yesterday and the day before, when Thy candle shined upon his head,[2] and he walked under the shadow of Thy wings,[3] from the temptations which beset him.

3. O Father, righteous and ever to be praised, the hour cometh

when Thy servant is to be proved. O beloved Father, it is well that in this hour Thy servant suffer somewhat for Thy sake. O Father, evermore to be adored, as the hour cometh which Thou foreknewest from everlasting, when for a little while Thy servant should outwardly bow down, but always live inwardly with Thee; when for a little while he should be little regarded, humbled, and fail in the eyes of men; should be wasted with sufferings and weaknesses, to rise again with Thee in the dawn of the new light, and be glorified in the heavenly places. O Holy Father, thou hast ordained it so, and so hast willed it; and that is done which Thou Thyself hast commanded.

4. For this is Thy favour to Thy friend, that he should suffer and be troubled in the world for Thy love's sake, how often soever, and by whomsoever and whosoever Thou hast suffered it to be done. Without Thy counsel and providence, and without cause, nothing cometh to pass on the earth. It is good for me, Lord, that I had been in trouble, that I may learn Thy statutes,(4) and may cast away all pride of heart and presumption. It is profitable for me that confusion hath covered my face, that I may seek to Thee for consolation rather than unto men. By this also I have learned to dread Thine unsearchable judgment, who afflictest the just with the wicked, but not without equity and justice.

5. Thanks be unto Thee, because Thou hast not spared my sins, but hast beaten me with stripes of love, inflicting pains, and sending troubles upon me without and within. There is none who can console me, of all things which are under heaven, but Thou only, O Lord my God, Thou heavenly Physician of souls, who dost scourge and hast mercy, who leadest down to hell and bringest up again.(5) Thy discipline over me, and Thy rod itself shall teach me.

6. Behold, O beloved Father, I am in Thy hands, I bow myself under the rod of Thy correction. Smite my back and my neck that I may bend my crookedness to Thy will. Make me a pious and lowly disciple, as Thou wert wont to be kind, that I may walk according to every nod of Thine. To Thee I commend myself and all that I have for correction; better is it to be punished here than hereafter. Thou knowest all things and each of them; and nothing

remaineth hid from Thee in man's conscience. Before they are, thou knowest that they will be, and Thou needest not that any man teach Thee or admonish Thee concerning the things which are done upon the earth. Thou knowest what is expedient for my profit, and how greatly trouble serveth unto the scrubbing off the rust of sin. Do with me according to Thy desired good pleasure, and despise not my life which is full of sin, known to none so entirely and fully as to Thee alone.

7. Grant me, O Lord, to know that which ought to be known; to love that which ought to be loved; to praise that which pleaseth Thee most, to esteem that which is precious in Thy sight, to blame that which is vile in Thine eyes. Suffer me not to judge according to the sight of bodily eyes, nor to give sentence according to the hearing of the ears of ignorant men; but to discern in true judgment between visible and spiritual things, and above all things to be ever seeking after the will of Thy good pleasure.

8. Oftentimes the senses of men are deceived in judging; the lovers of the world also are deceived in that they love only visible things. What is a man better because by man he is reckoned very great? The deceiver deceiveth the deceiver, the vain man the vain, the blind man the blind, the weak man the weak, when they exalt one another; and in truth they rather put to shame, while they foolishly praise. For as humble St. Francis saith, "What each one is in Thine eyes, so much he is, and no more."

(1) Psalm lxxxviii. 15.   (2) Job xxix. 3.   (3) Psalm xvii. 8.
(4) Psalm cxix. 71.   (5) Job xiii. 2.

CHAPTER LI

That we must give ourselves to humble works when we are unequal to those that are lofty

"My Son, thou art not always able to continue in very fervent desire after virtues, nor to stand fast in the loftier region of contemplation; but thou must of necessity sometimes descend to lower things because of thine original corruption, and bear about the burden of corruptible life, though unwillingly and with weariness. So long as thou wearest a mortal body, thou shalt feel weariness and heaviness of heart. Therefore thou oughtest to groan often in the flesh because of the burden of the flesh, inasmuch as thou canst not give thyself to spiritual studies and divine contemplation unceasingly.

2. "At such a time it is expedient for thee to flee to humble and external works, and to renew thyself with good actions; to wait for My coming and heavenly visitation with sure confidence; to bear thy exile and drought of mind with patience, until thou be visited by Me again, and be freed from all anxieties. For I will cause thee to forget thy labours, and altogether to enjoy eternal peace. I will spread open before thee the pleasant pastures of the Scriptures, that with enlarged heart thou mayest begin to run in the way of My commandments. And thou shalt say, 'The sufferings of this present time are not worthy to be compared with the glory which shall be revealed in us.'"(1)

(1) Romans viii. 18.

CHAPTER LII

That a man ought not to reckon himself worthy of consolation, but more worthy of chastisement

O Lord, I am not worthy of Thy consolation, nor of any spiritual visitation; and therefore Thou dealest justly with me, when Thou leavest me poor and desolate. For if I were able to pour forth tears like the sea, still should I not be worthy of Thy consolation. Therefore am I nothing worthy save to be scourged and punished, because I have grievously and many a time offended Thee, and in many things have greatly sinned. Therefore, true account being taken, I am not worthy even of the least of Thy consolations. But Thou, gracious and merciful God, who willest not that Thy works should perish, to show forth the riches of Thy mercy upon the vessels of mercy,(1) vouchsafest even beyond all his own deserving, to comfort Thy servant above the measure of mankind. For Thy consolations are not like unto the discoursings of men.

2. What have I done, O Lord, that Thou shouldst bestow any heavenly comfort upon me? I remember not that I have done any good, but have been ever prone to sin and slow to amendment. It is true and I cannot deny it. If I should say otherwise, Thou wouldst rise up against me, and there would be none to defend me. What have I deserved for my sins but hell and everlasting fire? In very truth I confess that I am worthy of all scorn and contempt, nor is it fit that I should be remembered among Thy faithful servants. And although I be unwilling to hear this, nevertheless I will for the Truth's sake, accuse myself of my sins, that the more readily I may prevail to be accounted worthy of Thy mercy.

3. What shall I say, guilty that I am and filled with confusion? I have no mouth to utter, unless it be this word alone, "I have sinned, Lord, I have sinned; have mercy upon me, forgive me." Let me alone, that I may take comfort a little before I go whence I shall not return even to the land of darkness and the shadow of death.(2) What dost Thou so much require of a guilty and miserable sinner, as that he be contrite, and humble himself for his sins? In true contrition and humiliation of heart is begotten the hope of pardon, the troubled conscience is reconciled, lost grace is recovered, a man is preserved from the wrath to come, and God and the penitent soul hasten to meet each other with a holy kiss.(3)

4. The humble contrition of sinners is an acceptable sacrifice unto Thee, O Lord, sending forth a smell sweeter far in Thy sight than the incense. This also is that pleasant ointment which Thou wouldst have poured upon Thy sacred feet, for a broken and contrite heart Thou hast never despised.(4) There is the place of refuge from the wrathful countenance of the enemy. There is amended and washed away whatsoever evil hath elsewhere been contracted.

(1) Romans ix. 23.   (2) Job x. 20, 21.   (3) Luke xv. 20.
(4) Psalm li. 17.

CHAPTER LIII

That the Grace of God doth not join itself to those who mind earthly things

"My Son, precious is My grace, it suffereth not itself to be joined with outward things, nor with earthly consolations. Therefore thou oughtest to cast away all things which hinder grace, if thou longest to receive the inpouring thereof. Seek a secret place for thyself, love to dwell alone with thyself, desire the conversation of no one; but rather pour out thy devout prayer to God, that thou mayest possess a contrite mind and a pure conscience. Count the whole world as nought; seek to be alone with God before all outward things. For thou canst not be alone with Me, and at the same time be delighted with transitory things. Thou oughtest to be separated from thy acquaintances and dear friends, and keep thy mind free from all worldly comfort. So the blessed Apostle Peter beseecheth, that Christ's faithful ones bear themselves in this world as strangers and pilgrims.(1)

2. "Oh how great a confidence shall there be to the dying man whom no affection to anything detaineth in the world? But to have a heart so separated from all things, a sickly soul doth not yet comprehend, nor doth the carnal man know the liberty of the spiritual man. But if indeed he desire to be spiritually minded, he must renounce both those who are far off, and those who are near, and to beware of no man more than himself. If thou perfectly conquer thyself, very easily shalt thou subdue all things besides. Perfect victory is the triumph over oneself. For whoso keepeth himself in subjection, in such manner that the sensual affections obey the reason, and the reason in all things obeyeth Me, he truly is conqueror of himself, and lord of the world.

3. "If thou desire to climb to this height, thou oughtest to start bravely, and to lay the axe to the root, to the end that thou mayest pull up and destroy the hidden inordinate inclination towards thyself, and towards all selfish and earthly good. From this sin, that a man loveth himself too inordinately, almost everything hangeth which needeth to be utterly overcome: when that evil is conquered and put under foot, there shall be great

peace and tranquillity continually. But because few strive earnestly to die perfectly to themselves, and do not heartily go forth from themselves, therefore do they remain entangled in themselves, and cannot be raised in spirit above themselves. But he who desireth to walk at liberty with Me, must of necessity mortify all his evil and inordinate affections, and must cling to no creature with selfish love."

(1) 1 Peter ii. 11.

CHAPTER LIV

Of the diverse motions of Nature and of Grace

"My Son, pay diligent heed to the motions of Nature and of Grace, because they move in a very contrary and subtle manner, and are hardly distinguished save by a spiritual and inwardly enlightened man. All men indeed seek good, and make pretence of something good in all that they say or do; and thus under the appearance of good many are deceived.

2. "Nature is deceitful and draweth away, ensnareth, and deceiveth many, and always hath self for her end; but Grace walketh in simplicity and turneth away from every appearance of evil, maketh no false pretences, and doeth all entirely for the sake of God, in whom also she finally resteth.

3. "Nature is very unwilling to die, and to be pressed down, and to be overcome, and to be in subjection, and to bear the yoke readily; but Grace studieth self-mortification, resisteth sensuality, seeketh to be subdued, longeth to be conquered, and willeth not to use her own liberty. She loveth to be held by discipline, and not to have authority over any, but always to live, to remain, to have her being under God, and for God's sake is ready to be humbly subject to every ordinance of man.

4. "Nature laboureth for her own advantage, and considereth what profit she may gain from another; but Grace considereth more, not what may be useful and convenient to self, but what may be profitable to the many.

5. "Nature willingly receiveth honour and reverence; but Grace faithfully ascribeth all honour and glory to God.

6. "Nature feareth confusion and contempt, but Grace rejoiceth to suffer shame for the name of Jesus.

7. "Nature loveth ease and bodily quiet; Grace cannot be unemployed, but gladly embraceth labour.

8. "Nature seeketh to possess things curious and attractive, and abhorreth those which are rough and cheap; Grace is delighted with things simple and humble, despiseth not those which are rough, nor refuseth to be clothed with old garments.

9. "Nature hath regard to things temporal, rejoiceth in earthly lucre, is made sad by loss, vexed by any little injurious word; but Grace reacheth after things eternal, cleaveth not to those which are temporal, is not perturbed by losses, nor embittered by any hard words, because she hath placed her treasure and joy in heaven where nought perisheth.

10. "Nature is covetous, and receiveth more willingly than she giveth, loveth things that are personal and private to herself; while Grace is kind and generous, avoideth selfishness, is contented with a little, believeth that it is more blessed to give than to receive.

11. "Nature inclineth thee to created things, to thine own flesh, to vanities and dissipation; but Grace draweth to God and to virtues, renounceth creatures, fleeth from the world, hateth the desires of the flesh, restraineth vagaries, blusheth to be seen in public.

12. "Nature is glad to receive some outward solace in which the senses may have delight; but Grace seeketh to be comforted in God alone, and to have delight in the chief good above all visible things.

13. "Nature doeth everything for her own gain and profit, can do nothing as a free favour, but hopeth to attain something as good

or better, or some praise or favour for her benefits; and she loveth that her own deeds and gifts should be highly valued; but Grace seeketh nothing temporal, nor requireth any other gift of reward than God alone; neither longeth she for more of temporal necessities than such as may suffice for the attaining of eternal life.

14. "Nature rejoiceth in many friends and kinsfolk, she boasteth of noble place and noble birth, she smileth on the powerful, flattereth the rich, applaudeth those who are like herself; but Grace loveth even her enemies, and is not lifted up by the multitude of friends, setteth no store upon high place or high birth, unless there be greater virtue therewith; favoureth the poor man more than the rich, hath more sympathy with the innocent than with the powerful; rejoiceth with the truthful, not with the liar; always exhorteth the good to strive after better gifts of grace, and to become by holiness like unto the Son of God.

15. "Nature quickly complaineth of poverty and of trouble; Grace beareth want with constancy.

16. "Nature looketh upon all things in reference to herself; striveth and argueth for self; but Grace bringeth back all things to God from whom they came at the beginning; ascribeth no good to herself nor arrogantly presumeth; is not contentious, nor preferreth her own opinion to others, but in every sense and understanding submitteth herself to the Eternal wisdom and the Divine judgment.

17. "Nature is eager to know secrets and to hear new things; she loveth to appear abroad, and to make experience of many things through the senses; she desireth to be acknowledged and to do those things which win praise and admiration; but Grace careth not to gather up new or curious things, because all this springeth from the old corruption, whereas there is nothing new or lasting upon earth. So she teacheth to restrain the senses, to shun vain complacency and ostentation, to hide humbly those things which merit praise and real admiration, and from everything and in all knowledge to seek after useful fruit, and the praise and honour of God. She desireth not to receive praise for herself or her own, but longeth that God be blessed in all

His gifts, who out of unmingled love bestoweth all things."

18. This Grace is a supernatural light, and a certain special gift of God, and the proper mark of the elect, and the pledge of eternal salvation; it exalteth a man from earthly things to love those that are heavenly; and it maketh the carnal man spiritual. So far therefore as Nature is utterly pressed down and overcome, so far is greater Grace bestowed and the inner man is daily created anew by fresh visitations, after the image of God.

CHAPTER LV

Of the corruption of Nature and the efficacy of Divine Grace

O Lord my God, who hast created me after thine own image and similitude, grant me this grace, which Thou hast shown to be so great and so necessary for salvation, that I may conquer my wicked nature, which draweth me to sin and to perdition. For I feel in my flesh the law of sin, contradicting the law of my mind, and bringing me into captivity to the obedience of sensuality in many things; nor can I resist its passions, unless Thy most holy grace assist me, fervently poured into my heart.

2. There is need of Thy grace, yea, and of a great measure thereof, that my nature may be conquered, which hath alway been prone to evil from my youth. For being fallen through the first man Adam, and corrupted through sin, the punishment of this stain descended upon all men; so that Nature itself, which was framed good and right by Thee, is now used to express the vice and infirmity of corrupted Nature; because its motion left unto itself draweth men away to evil and to lower things. For the little power which remaineth is as it were one spark lying hid in the ashes. This is Natural reason itself, encompassed with thick clouds, having yet a discernment of good and evil, a distinction of the true and the false, though it be powerless to fulfil all that it approveth, and possess not yet the full light of truth, nor healthfulness of its affections.

3. Hence it is, O my God, that I delight in Thy law after the inward man,(1) knowing that Thy commandment is holy and just and

good; reproving also all evil, and the sin that is to be avoided: yet with the flesh I serve the law of sin, whilst I obey sensuality rather than reason. Hence it is that to will to do good is present with me, but how to perform it I find not.(2) Hence I ofttimes purpose many good things; but because grace is lacking to help mine infirmities, I fall back before a little resistance and fail. Hence it cometh to pass that I recognize the way of perfectness, and see very clearly what things I ought to do; but pressed down by the weight of my own corruption, I rise not to the things which are more perfect.

4. Oh how entirely necessary is Thy grace to me, O Lord, for a good beginning, for progress, and for bringing to perfection. For without it I can do nothing, but I can do all things through Thy grace which strengtheneth me.(3) O truly heavenly grace, without which our own merits are nought, and no gifts of Nature at all are to be esteemed. Arts, riches, beauty, strength, wit, eloquence, they all avail nothing before Thee, O Lord, without Thy grace. For the gifts of Nature belong to good and evil alike; but the proper gift of the elect is grace--that is, love-- and they who bear the mark thereof are held worthy of everlasting life. So mighty is this grace, that without it neither the gift of prophecy nor the working of miracles, nor any speculation, howsoever lofty, is of any value at all. But neither faith, nor hope, nor any other virtue is accepted with Thee without love and grace.

5. O most blessed grace that makest the poor in spirit rich in virtues, and renderest him who is rich in many things humble in spirit, come Thou, descend upon me, fill me early with Thy consolation, lest my soul fail through weariness and drought of mind. I beseech thee, O Lord, that I may find grace in Thy sight, for Thy grace is sufficient for me,(4) when I obtain not those things which Nature longeth for. If I be tempted and vexed with many tribulations, I will fear no evil, while Thy grace remaineth with me. This alone is my strength, this bringeth me counsel and help. It is more powerful than all enemies, and wiser than all the wise men in the world.

6. It is the mistress of truth, the teacher of discipline, the light of the heart, the solace of anxiety, the banisher of

sorrow, the deliverer from fear, the nurse of devotion, the drawer forth of tears. What am I without it, save a dry tree, a useless branch, worthy to be cast away! "Let Thy grace, therefore, O Lord, always prevent and follow me, and make me continually given to all good works, through Jesus Christ, Thy Son. Amen."

(1) Romans vii. 12, 22. 25. (2) Romans vii. 18. (3) Philippians iv. 13. (4) 2 Corinthians xii. 9.

CHAPTER LVI

That we ought to deny ourselves, and to imitate Christ by means of the Cross

My Son, so far as thou art able to go out of thyself so far shalt thou be able to enter into Me. As to desire no outward thing worketh internal peace, so the forsaking of self inwardly joineth unto God. I will that thou learn perfect self-denial, living in My will without contradiction or complaint. Follow Me: I am the way, the truth, and the life.(1) Without the way thou canst not go, without the truth thou canst not know, without the life thou canst not live. I am the Way which thou oughtest to follow; the Truth which thou oughtest to believe; the Life which thou oughtest to hope for. I am the Way unchangeable; the Truth infallible; the Life everlasting. I am the Way altogether straight, the Truth supreme, the true Life, the blessed Life, the uncreated Life. If thou remain in My way thou shalt know the Truth, and the truth shall make thee free,(2) and thou shalt lay hold on eternal life.

2. "If thou wilt enter into life, keep the commandments.(3) If thou wilt know the truth, believe in Me. If thou wilt be perfect, sell all that thou hast. If thou wilt be My disciple, deny thyself. If thou wouldst possess the blessed life, despise the life which now is. If thou wilt be exalted in heaven, humble thyself in the world. If thou wilt reign with Me, bear the cross with Me; for only the servants of the cross find the way of blessedness and of true light."

3. O Lord Jesu, forasmuch as Thy life was straitened and despised

by the world, grant unto me to imitate Thee in despising the world, for the servant is not greater than his lord, nor the disciple above his master.(4) Let Thy servant be exercised in Thy life, because there is my salvation and true holiness. Whatsoever I read or hear besides it, it refresheth me not, nor giveth me delight.

4. "My son, because thou knowest these things and hast read them all, blessed shalt thou be if thou doest them. He who hath My commandments and keepeth them, he it is that loveth Me, and I will love him, and will manifest Myself to him,(5) and I will make him to sit down with Me in My Father's Kingdom."

5. O Lord Jesu, as Thou hast said and promised, even so let it be unto me, and grant me to prove worthy. I have received the cross at Thy hand; I have carried it, and will carry it even unto death, as Thou hast laid it upon me. Truly the life of a truly devoted servant is a cross, but it leadeth to paradise. I have begun; I may not return back nor leave it.

6. Come, my brothers, let us together go forward. Jesus shall be with us. For Jesus' sake have we taken up this cross, for Jesus' sake let us persevere in the cross. He will be our helper, who was our Captain and Forerunner. Behold our King entereth in before us, and He will fight for us. Let us follow bravely, let no man fear terrors; let us be prepared to die bravely in battle, and let us not so stain our honour,(6) as to fly from the cross.

(1) John xiv. 6.   (2) John viii. 32.   (3) Matthew xix. 17, 21.
(4) Matthew x. 24.   (5) John xiv. 21.   (6) 1 Mac. ix. 10.

CHAPTER LVII

That a man must not be too much cast down when he falleth into some faults

"My Son, patience and humility in adversities are more pleasing to Me than much comfort and devotion in prosperity. Why doth a little thing spoken against thee make thee sad? If it had been more, thou still oughtest not to be moved. But now suffer it to go by; it is not the first, it is not new, and it will not be the last, if thou live long. Thou art brave enough, so long as no adversity meeteth thee. Thou givest good counsel also, and knowest how to strengthen others with thy words; but when tribulation suddenly knocketh at thine own door, thy counsel and strength fail. Consider thy great frailty, which thou dost so often experience in trifling matters nevertheless, for thy soul's health these things are done when they and such like happen unto thee.

2. "Put them away from thy heart as well as thou canst, and if tribulation hath touched thee, yet let it not cast thee down nor entangle thee long. At the least, bear patiently, if thou canst not joyfully. And although thou be very unwilling to hear it, and feel indignation, yet check thyself, and suffer no unadvised word to come forth from thy lips, whereby the little ones may be offended. Soon the storm which hath been raised shall be stilled, and inward grief shall be sweetened by returning grace. I yet live, saith the Lord, ready to help thee, and to give thee more than wonted consolation if thou put thy trust in Me, and call devoutly upon Me.

3. "Be thou more calm of spirit, and gird thyself for greater endurance. All is not frustrated, though thou find thyself very often afflicted or grievously tempted. Thou art man, not God; thou art flesh, not an angel. How shouldst thou be able to remain alway in the same state of virtue, when an angel in heaven fell, and the first man in paradise? I am He who lifteth up the mourners to deliverance, and those who know their own infirmity I raise up to my own nature."

4. O Lord, blessed be Thy word, sweeter to my mouth than honey and the honeycomb. What should I do in my so great tribulations and anxieties, unless Thou didst comfort me with Thy holy words? If only I may attain unto the haven of salvation, what matter is it what things or how many I suffer? Give me a good end, give me a happy passage out of this world. Remember me, O my God, and lead me by the right way unto Thy Kingdom. Amen.

CHAPTER LVIII

Of deeper matters, and God's hidden judgments which are not to be inquired into

"My Son, beware thou dispute not of high matters and of the hidden judgments of God; why this man is thus left, and that man is taken into so great favour; why also this man is so greatly afflicted, and that so highly exalted. These things pass all man's power of judging, neither may any reasoning or disputation have power to search out the divine judgments. When therefore the enemy suggesteth these things to thee, or when any curious people ask such questions, answer with that word of the Prophet, Just art Thou, O Lord, and true is Thy judgment,(1) and with this, The judgments of the Lord are true, and righteous altogether.(2) My judgments are to be feared, not to be disputed on, because they are incomprehensible to human understanding.

2. "And be not given to inquire or dispute about the merits of the Saints, which is holier than another, or which is the greater in the Kingdom of Heaven. Such questions often beget useless strifes and contentions: they also nourish pride and vain glory, whence envyings and dissensions arise, while one man arrogantly endeavoureth to exalt one Saint and another another. But to wish to know and search out such things bringeth no fruit, but it rather displeaseth the Saints; for I am not the God of confusion but of peace;(3) which peace consisteth more in true humility than in self-exaltation.

3. "Some are drawn by zeal of love to greater affection to these Saints or those; but this is human affection rather than divine. I am He Who made all the Saints: I gave them grace, I brought them glory; I know the merits of every one; I prevented them with the blessings of My goodness.(4) I foreknew my beloved ones from everlasting, I chose them out of the world;(5) they did not choose Me. I called them by My grace, drew them by My mercy, led them on through sundry temptations. I poured mighty consolations upon them, I gave them perseverance, I crowned their patience.

4. "I acknowledge the first and the last; I embrace all with inestimable love. I am to be praised in all My Saints; I am to

be blessed above all things, and to be honoured in every one whom I have so gloriously exalted and predestined, without any preceding merits of their own. He therefore that shall despise one of the least of these My people, honoureth not the great; because I made both small and great.(6) And he who speaketh against any of My Saints speaketh against Me, and against all others in the Kingdom of Heaven."

They are all one through the bond of charity; they think the same thing, will the same thing, and all are united in love one to another.

5. "But yet (which is far better) they love Me above themselves and their own merits. For being caught up above themselves, and drawn beyond self-love, they go all straightforward to the love of Me, and they rest in Me in perfect enjoyment. There is nothing which can turn them away or press them down; for being full of Eternal Truth, they burn with the fire of inextinguishable charity. Therefore let all carnal and natural men hold their peace concerning the state of the Saints, for they know nothing save to love their own personal enjoyment. They take away and add according to their own inclination, not as it pleaseth the Eternal Truth.

6. "In many men this is ignorance, chiefly is it so in those who, being little enlightened, rarely learn to love any one with perfect spiritual love. They are still much drawn by natural affection and human friendship to these or to those: and as they reckon of themselves in lower matters, so also do they frame imaginations of things heavenly. But there is an immeasurable difference between those things which they imperfectly imagine, and these things which enlightened men behold through supernatural revelation.

7. "Take heed, therefore, My son, that thou treat not curiously those things which surpass thy knowledge, but rather make this thy business and give attention to it, namely, that thou seek to be found, even though it be the least, in the Kingdom of God. And even if any one should know who were holier than others, or who were held greatest in the Kingdom of Heaven; what should that knowledge profit him, unless through this knowledge he should

humble himself before Me, and should rise up to give greater praise unto My name? He who considereth how great are his own sins, how small his virtues, and how far he is removed from the perfection of the Saints, doeth far more acceptably in the sight of God, than he who disputeth about their greatness or littleness.

8. "They are altogether well content, if men would learn to be content, and to refrain from vain babbling. They glory not of their own merits, seeing they ascribe no good unto themselves, but all unto Me, seeing that I of my infinite charity have given them all things. They are filled with so great love of the Divinity, and with such overflowing joy, that no glory is lacking to them, neither can any felicity be lacking. All the Saints, the higher they are exalted in glory, the humbler are they in themselves, and the nearer and dearer are they unto Me. And so thou hast it written that they cast their crowns before God and fell on their faces before the Lamb, and worshipped Him that liveth for ever and ever.(7)

9. "Many ask who is greatest in the Kingdom of Heaven, who know not whether they shall be worthy to be counted among the least. It is a great thing to be even the least in Heaven, where all are great, because all shall be called, and shall be, the sons of God. A little one shall become a thousand, but the sinner being an hundred years old shall be accursed. For when the disciples asked who should be the greatest in the Kingdom of Heaven, they received no other answer than this, Except ye be converted and become as little children, ye shall not enter into the Kingdom of Heaven. But whosoever shall humble himself as this little child, the same shall be greatest in the Kingdom of Heaven."(8)

10. Woe unto them who disdain to humble themselves willingly with the little children; for the low gate of the kingdom of Heaven will not suffer them to enter in. Woe also to them who are rich, who have their consolation here;(9) because whilst the poor enter into the kingdom of God, they shall stand lamenting without. Rejoice ye humble, and exult ye poor, for yours is the kingdom of God if only ye walk in the truth.

(1) Psalm cxix. 137. (2) Psalm xix. 9.

(3) Corinthians xiv. 33.   (4) Psalm xxi. 3.   (5) John xv. 19.
(6) Wisd. vi. 8.   (7) Revelation iv. 10; v. 14.
(8) Matthew xviii. 3.   (9) Philippians ii. 21.

CHAPTER LIX

That all hope and trust is to be fixed in God alone

O Lord, what is my trust which I have in this life, or what is my greatest comfort of all the things which are seen under Heaven? Is it not Thou, O Lord my God, whose mercies are without number? Where hath it been well with me without Thee? Or when could it be evil whilst Thou wert near? I had rather be poor for Thy sake, than rich without Thee. I choose rather to be a pilgrim upon the earth with Thee than without Thee to possess heaven. Where Thou art, there is heaven; and where Thou are not, behold there death and hell. Thou art all my desire, and therefore must I groan and cry and earnestly pray after Thee. In short I can confide fully in none to give me ready help in necessities, save in Thee alone, O my God. Thou art my hope, Thou art my trust, Thou art my Comforter, and most faithful in all things.

2. All men seek their own;(1) Thou settest forward only my salvation and my profit, and turnest all things unto my good. Even though Thou dost expose me to divers temptations and adversities, Thou ordainest all this unto my advantage, for Thou are wont to prove Thy beloved ones in a thousand ways. In which proving Thou oughtest no less to be loved and praised, than if Thou wert filling me full of heavenly consolations.

3. In Thee, therefore, O Lord God, I put all my hope and my refuge, on Thee I lay all my tribulation and anguish; because I find all to be weak and unstable whatsoever I behold out of Thee. For many friends shall not profit, nor strong helpers be able to succour, nor prudent counsellors to give a useful answer, nor the books of the learned to console, nor any precious substance to deliver, nor any secret and beautiful place to give shelter, if Thou Thyself do not assist, help, strengthen, comfort, instruct, keep in safety.

4. For all things which seem to belong to the attainment of peace and felicity are nothing when Thou art absent, and bring no felicity at all in reality. Therefore art Thou the end of all good, and the fulness of Life, and the soul of eloquence; and to hope in Thee above all things is the strongest solace of Thy servants. Mine eyes look unto Thee,(2) in Thee is my trust, O my God, Father of mercies.

5. Bless and sanctify my soul with heavenly blessing that it may become Thy holy habitation, and the seat of Thy eternal glory; and let nothing be found in the Temple of Thy divinity which may offend the eyes of Thy majesty. According to the greatness of Thy goodness and the multitude of Thy mercies look upon me, and hear the prayer of Thy poor servant, far exiled from Thee in the land of the shadow of death. Protect and preserve the soul of Thy least servant amid so many dangers of corruptible life, and by Thy grace accompanying me, direct it by the way of peace unto its home of perpetual light. Amen.

(1) Luke vi.   (2) Psalm cxli. 8.

THE FOURTH BOOK

OF THE SACRAMENT OF THE ALTAR

A devout exhortation to the Holy Communion

The Voice of Christ

Come unto Me, all ye that labour and are heavy laden, and I will refresh you,(1) saith the Lord. The bread that I will give is My flesh which I give for the life of the world.(2) Take, eat: this is My Body, which is given for you; this do in remembrance of Me.(3) He that eateth My flesh and drinketh My blood dwelleth in Me and I in him. The words that I speak unto you, they are spirit, and they are life.(4)

(1) Matthew xi. 28   (2) John vi. 51.
(3) Matthew xxi. 26; Luke xxii. 19.   (4) John vi. 51, 63.

CHAPTER I

With how great reverence Christ must be received

The Voice of the Disciple

These are Thy words, O Christ, Eternal Truth; though not uttered at one time nor written together in one place of Scripture. Because therefore they are Thy words and true, I must gratefully and faithfully receive them all. They are Thine, and Thou hast uttered them; and they are mine also, because Thou didst speak them for my salvation. Gladly I receive them from Thy mouth, that they may be more deeply implanted in my heart. Words of such great grace arouse me, for they are full of sweetness and love; but my own sins terrify me, and my impure conscience driveth me away from receiving so great mysteries. The sweetness of Thy words encourageth me, but the multitude of my faults presseth me down.

2. Thou commandest that I draw near to Thee with firm confidence, if I would have part with Thee, and that I receive the food of immortality, if I desire to obtain eternal life and glory. Come unto Me, sayest Thou, all that labour and are heavy laden, and I will refresh you. Oh, sweet and lovely word in the ear of the sinner, that Thou, O Lord my God, dost invite the poor and needy to the Communion of Thy most holy body and blood. But who am I, O Lord, that I should presume to approach unto Thee? Behold the heaven of heavens cannot contain Thee, and yet Thou sayest, Come ye all unto Me.

3. What meaneth this most gracious condescension, this most lovely invitation? How shall I dare to come, who know no good thing of myself, whence I might be able to presume? How shall I bring Thee within my house, seeing that I so often have sinned in Thy most loving sight? Angels and Archangels stand in awe of Thee, the Saints and just men fear Thee, and Thou sayest, Come

unto Me! Except Thou, Lord, hadst said it, who should believe it true? And except Thou hadst commanded, who should attempt to draw near?

4. Behold, Noah, that just man, laboured for a hundred years in building the ark, that he might be saved with the few; and I, how shall I be able in one hour to prepare myself to receive the Builder of the world with reverence? Moses, Thy servant, Thy great and especial friend, made an ark of incorruptible wood, which also he covered with purest gold, that he might lay up in it the tables of the law, and I, a corruptible creature, shall I dare thus easily to receive Thee, the Maker of the Law and the Giver of life? Solomon, the wisest of the kings of Israel, was seven years building his magnificent temple to the praise of Thy Name, and for eight days celebrated the feast of its dedication, offered a thousand peace offerings, and solemnly brought up the Ark of the Covenant to the place prepared for it, with the sound of trumpets and great joy, and I, unhappy and poorest of mankind, how shall I bring Thee into my house, who scarce know how to spend half an hour in devotion? And oh that it were even one half hour worthily spent!

5. O my God, how earnestly these holy men strove to please Thee! And alas! how little and trifling is that which I do! how short a time do I spend, when I am disposing myself to Communion. Rarely altogether collected, most rarely cleansed from all distraction. And surely in the saving presence of Thy Godhead no unmeet thought ought to intrude, nor should any creature take possession of me, because it is not an Angel but the Lord of the Angels, that I am about to receive as my Guest.

6. Yet there is a vast difference between the Ark of the Covenant with its relics, and Thy most pure Body with its ineffable virtues, between those sacrifices of the law, which were figures of things to come, and the true sacrifice of Thy Body, the completion of all the ancient sacrifices.

7. Wherefore then do I not yearn more ardently after Thy adorable presence? Why do I not prepare myself with greater solicitude to receive Thy holy things, when those holy Patriarchs and Prophets of old, kings also and princes, with the whole people, manifested

so great affection of devotion towards Thy Divine Service?

8. The most devout king David danced with all his might before the Ark of God, calling to mind the benefits granted to his forefathers in days past; he fashioned musical instruments of various sorts, put forth Psalms, and appointed them to be sung with joy, played also himself ofttimes on the harp, being inspired with the grace of the Holy Ghost; he taught the people of Israel to praise God with the whole heart, and with unity of voice to bless and praise Him every day. If so great devotion was then exercised, and celebration of divine praise was carried on before the Ark of the Testimony, how great reverence and devotion ought now to be shown by me and all Christian people at the ministering of the Sacrament, at receiving the most precious Body and Blood of Christ.

9. Many run to diverse places to visit the memorials of departed Saints, and rejoice to hear of their deeds and to look upon the beautiful buildings of their shrines. And behold, Thou art present here with me, O my God, Saint of Saints, Creator of men and Lord of the Angels. Often in looking at those memorials men are moved by curiosity and novelty, and very little fruit of amendment is borne away, especially when there is so much careless trifling and so little true contrition. But here in the Sacrament of the Altar, Thou art present altogether, My God, the Man Christ Jesus; where also abundant fruit of eternal life is given to every one soever that receiveth Thee worthily and devoutly. But to this no levity draweth, no curiosity, nor sensuality, only steadfast faith, devout hope, and sincere charity.

10. O God, invisible Creator of the world, how wondrously dost Thou work with us, how sweetly and graciously Thou dealest with Thine elect, to whom Thou offerest Thyself to be received in this Sacrament! For this surpasseth all understanding, this specially draweth the hearts of the devout and enkindleth their affections. For even thy true faithful ones themselves, who order their whole life to amendment, oftentimes gain from this most excellent Sacrament great grace of devotion and love of virtue.

11. Oh admirable and hidden grace of the Sacrament, which only

Christ's faithful ones know, but the faithless and those who serve sin cannot experience! In this Sacrament is conferred spiritual grace, and lost virtue is regained in the soul, and the beauty which was disfigured by sin returneth again. So great sometimes is this grace that out of the fulness of devotion given, not only the mind but also the weak body feeleth that more strength is supplied unto it.

12. But greatly must we mourn and lament over our lukewarmness and negligence, that we are not drawn by greater affection to become partakers of Christ, in whom all the hope and the merit of those that are to be saved consist. For He Himself is our sanctification and redemption.(1) He is the consolation of pilgrims and the eternal fruition of the Saints. Therefore it is grievously to be lamented that many so little consider this health-giving mystery, which maketh heaven glad and preserveth the whole world. Alas for the blindness and hardness of man's heart, that he considereth not more this unspeakable gift, and even slippeth down through the daily use, into carelessness.

13. For if this most holy Sacrament were celebrated in one place only, and were consecrated only by one priest in the whole world, with what great desire thinkest thou, would men be affected towards that place and towards such a priest of God, that they might behold the divine mysteries celebrated? But now are many men made priests and in many places the Sacrament is celebrated, that the grace and love of God towards men might the more appear, the more widely the Holy Communion is spread abroad over all the world. Thanks be unto Thee, O good Jesus, Eternal Shepherd, who hast vouchsafed to refresh us, poor and exiled ones, with Thy precious Body and Blood, and to invite us to partake these holy mysteries by the invitation from Thine own mouth, saying, Come unto Me, ye who labour and are heavy laden, and I will refresh you.

(1) 1 Corinthians i. 30.

CHAPTER II

That the greatness and charity of God is shown to men in the Sacrament

The Voice of the Disciple

Trusting in Thy goodness and great mercy, O Lord, I draw near, the sick to the Healer, the hungering and thirsting to the Fountain of life, the poverty-stricken to the King of heaven, the servant to the Lord, the creature to the Creator, the desolate to my own gentle Comforter. But whence is this unto me, that Thou comest unto me? Who am I that Thou shouldest offer me Thyself? How doth a sinner dare to appear before Thee? And how dost thou vouchsafe to come to the sinner? Thou knowest Thy servant, and Thou knowest that he hath in him no good thing for which Thou shouldest grant him this grace. I confess therefore mine own vileness, I acknowledge Thy goodness, I praise Thy tenderness, and I give Thee thanks for Thine exceeding great love. For Thou doest this for Thine own sake, not for my merits, that Thy goodness may be more manifest unto me, Thy charity more abundantly poured out upon me, and Thy humility more perfectly commended unto me. Therefore because this pleaseth Thee and Thou hast commanded that thus it shall be, Thy condescension pleaseth me also; and oh that mine iniquity hinder it not.

2. O most sweet and tender Jesus, what reverence, what giving of thanks is due to Thee with perpetual praise for the receiving of Thy sacred Body and Blood, the dignity whereof no man is found able to express. But what shall I think upon in this Communion in approaching my Lord, whom I am not able worthily to honour, and nevertheless whom I long devoutly to receive? What shall be better and more healthful meditation for me, than utter humiliation of myself before Thee, and exaltation of Thine infinite goodness towards me? I praise Thee, O my God, and exalt Thee for evermore. I despise myself, and cast myself down before Thee into the deep of my vileness.

3. Behold, Thou art the Saint of saints and I the refuse of sinners; behold, Thou stoopest unto me who am not worthy to look upon Thee; behold, Thou comest unto me, Thou willest to be with

me, Thou invitest me to Thy feast. Thou willest to give me the heavenly food and bread of angels to eat; none other, in truth, than Thyself, The living bread, which didst descend from heaven; and givest life to the world.(1)

4. Behold, whence this love proceedeth! what manner of condescension shineth forth herein. What great giving of thanks and praise is due unto Thee for these benefits! Oh how salutary and profitable Thy purpose when Thou didst ordain this! How sweet and pleasant the feast when Thou didst give Thyself for food! Oh how admirable is thy working, O Lord, how mighty Thy power, how unspeakable Thy truth! For Thou didst speak the word, and all things were made; and this is done which Thou hast commanded.

5. A thing wonderful, and worthy of faith, and surpassing all the understanding of man, that Thou, O Lord my God, very God and very man, givest Thyself altogether to us in a little bread and wine, and art so our inexhaustible food. Thou, O Lord of all, who hast need of nothing, hast willed to dwell in us through Thy Sacrament. Preserve my heart and my body undefiled, that with a joyful and pure conscience I may be able very often to [celebrate, and](2) receive to my perpetual health. Thy mysteries, which Thou hast consecrated and instituted both for Thine own honour, and for a perpetual memorial.

6. Rejoice, O my soul, and give thanks unto God for so great a gift and precious consolation, left unto thee in this vale of tears. For so oft as thou callest this mystery to mind and receivest the body of Christ, so often dost thou celebrate the work of thy redemption, and art made partaker of all the merits of Christ. For the charity of Christ never groweth less, and the greatness of His propitiation is never exhausted. Therefore, by continual renewal of thy spirit, thou oughtest to dispose thyself hereunto and to weigh the great mystery of salvation with attentive consideration. So great, new, and joyful ought it to appear to thee when thou comest to communion, as if on this self-same day Christ for the first time were descending into the Virgin's womb and becoming man, or hanging on the cross, suffering and dying for the salvation of mankind.

(1) John vi. 51.
(2) The words in brackets are only suitable for a priest.

CHAPTER III

That it is profitable to Communicate often

The Voice of the Disciple

Behold I come unto Thee, O Lord, that I may be blessed through Thy gift, and be made joyful in Thy holy feast which Thou, O God, of Thy goodness hast prepared for the poor.(1) Behold in Thee is all that I can and ought to desire, Thou art my salvation and redemption, my hope and strength, my honour and glory. Therefore rejoice the soul of Thy servant this day, for unto Thee, O Lord Jesus, do I lift up my soul.(2) I long now to receive Thee devoutly and reverently, I desire to bring Thee into my house, so that with Zacchaeus I may be counted worthy to be blessed by Thee and numbered among the children of Abraham. My soul hath an earnest desire for Thy Body, my heart longeth to be united with Thee.

2. Give me Thyself and it sufficeth, for besides Thee no consolation availeth. Without Thee I cannot be, and without Thy visitation I have no power to live. And therefore I must needs draw nigh unto Thee often, and receive Thee for the healing of my soul, lest haply I faint by the way if I be deprived of heavenly food. For so Thou, most merciful Jesus, preaching to the people and healing many sick, didst once say, I will not send them away fasting to their own homes, lest they faint by the way.(3) Deal therefore now to me in like manner, for Thou left Thyself for the consolation of the faithful in the Sacrament. For Thou art the sweet refreshment of the soul, and he who shall eat Thee worthily shall be partaker and inheritor of the eternal glory. Necessary indeed it is for me, who so often slide backwards and sin, so quickly wax cold and faint, to renew, cleanse, enkindle myself by frequent prayers and penitences and receiving of Thy sacred Body and Blood lest haply by too long abstinence, I fall short of my holy resolutions.

3. For the imaginations of man's heart are evil from his youth,(4) and except divine medicine succour him, man slideth away continually unto the worse. The Holy Communion therefore draweth us back from evil, and strengtheneth us for good. For if I now be so negligent and lukewarm when I communicate [or celebrate], how should it be with me, if I receive not this medicine, and sought not so great a help? [And though I am not every day fit nor well prepared to celebrate, I will nevertheless give diligent heed at due season, to receive the divine mysteries, and to become partaker of so great grace]. For this is the one principal consolation of a faithful soul, so long as it is absent from Thee in mortal body, that being continually mindful of its God, it receiveth its Beloved with devout spirit.

4. Oh wonderful condescension of Thy pity surrounding us, that Thou, O Lord God, Creator and Quickener of all spirits, deignest to come unto a soul so poor and weak, and to appease its hunger with Thy whole Deity and Humanity. Oh happy mind and blessed soul, to which is granted devoutly to receive Thee its Lord God, and in so receiving Thee to be filled with all spiritual joy! Oh how great a Lord doth it entertain, how beloved a Guest doth it bring in, how delightful a Companion doth it receive, how faithful a Friend doth it welcome, how beautiful and exalted a Spouse, above every other Beloved, doth it embrace, One to be loved above all things that can be desired! Oh my most sweet Beloved, let heaven and earth and all the glory of them, be silent in Thy presence; seeing whatsoever praise and beauty they have it is of Thy gracious bounty; and they shall never reach unto the loveliness of Thy Name, Whose Wisdom is infinite.(5)

(1) Psalm lxviii. 10.   (2) Psalm lxxxvi. 4.
(3) Matthew xv. 32.   (4) Genesis viii. 21.
(5) Psalm cxlvii. 5.

CHAPTER IV

That many good gifts are bestowed upon those who Communicate devoutly

The Voice of the Disciple

O Lord my God, prevent Thou Thy servant with the blessings of Thy sweetness, that I may be enabled to draw near worthily and devoutly to Thy glorious Sacrament. Awaken my heart towards Thee, and deliver me from heavy slumber. Visit me with Thy salvation that I may in spirit taste Thy sweetness, which plentifully lieth hid in this Sacrament as in a fountain. Lighten also mine eyes to behold this so great mystery, and strengthen me that I may believe it with undoubting faith. For it is Thy word, not human power; it is Thy holy institution, not the invention of man. For no man is found fit in himself to receive and to understand these things, which transcend even the wisdom of the Angels. What portion then shall I, unworthy sinner, who am but dust and ashes, be able to search into and comprehend of so deep a Sacrament?

2. O Lord, in the simplicity of my heart, in good and firm faith, and according to Thy will, I draw nigh unto Thee with hope and reverence, and truly believe that Thou art here present in the Sacrament, God and man. Thou willest therefore that I receive Thee and unite myself to Thee in charity. Wherefore I beseech Thy mercy, and implore Thee to give me Thy special grace, to this end, that I may be wholly dissolved and overflow with love towards Thee, and no more suffer any other consolation to enter into me. For this most high and most glorious Sacrament is the health of the soul and the body, the medicine of all spiritual sickness, whereby I am healed of my sins, my passions are bridled, temptations are conquered or weakened, more grace is poured into me, virtue begun is increased, faith is made firm, hope is strengthened, and charity is enkindled and enlarged.

3. For in this Sacrament Thou hast bestowed many good things and still bestowest them continually on Thine elect who communicate devoutly, O my God, Lifter up of my soul, Repairer of human infirmity, and Giver of all inward consolation. For Thou pourest into them much consolation against all sorts of tribulation, and out of the deep of their own misery Thou liftest them up to the hope of Thy protection, and with ever new grace, dost inwardly refresh and enlighten them; so that they who felt themselves to be anxious and without affection before Communion, afterwards being refreshed with heavenly food and drink, find themselves

changed for the better. And even in such wise Thou dealest severally with Thine elect, that they may truly acknowledge and clearly make proof that they have nothing whatsoever of their own, and what goodness and grace come to them from Thee; because being in themselves cold, hard of heart, indevout, through Thee they become fervent, zealous, and devout. For who is there coming humbly to the fountain of sweetness, carrieth not away thence at the least some little of that sweetness? Or who standing by a large fire, feeleth not from thence a little of its heat? And Thou art ever a full and overflowing fountain, a fire continually burning, and never going out.

4. Wherefore if it is not suffered to me to draw from the fulness of the fountain, nor to drink unto satisfying, yet will I set my lips to the mouth of the heavenly conduit, that at least I may receive a small drop to quench my thirst, that I dry not up within my heart. And if I am not yet able to be altogether heavenly and so enkindled as the Cherubim and Seraphim, yet will I endeavour to give myself unto devotion, and to prepare my heart, that I may gain if it be but a little flame of the divine fire, through the humble receiving of the life-giving Sacrament. But whatsoever is wanting unto me, O merciful Jesus, Most Holy Saviour, do Thou of Thy kindness and grace supply, who hast vouchsafed to call all unto Thee, saying, Come unto me, all ye that are weary and heavy laden, and I will refresh you.

5. I indeed labour in the sweat of my face, I am tormented with sorrow of heart, I am burdened with sins, I am disquieted with temptations, I am entangled and oppressed with many passions, and there is none to help me, there is none to deliver and ease me, but Thou, O Lord God, my Saviour, to whom I commit myself and all things that are mine, that Thou mayest preserve me and lead me unto life eternal.

   Receive me unto the praise and glory of Thy name, who hast prepared Thy Body and Blood to be my meat and drink. Grant, O Lord God my Saviour, that with coming often to Thy mysteries the zeal of my devotion may increase.

CHAPTER V

Of the dignity of this Sacrament, and of the office of the priest

The Voice of the Beloved

If thou hadst angelic purity and the holiness of holy John the Baptist, thou wouldest not be worthy to receive or to minister this Sacrament. For this is not deserved by merit of man that a man should consecrate and minister the Sacrament of Christ, and take for food the bread of Angels. Vast is the mystery, and great is the dignity of the priests, to whom is given what is not granted to Angels. For priests only, rightly ordained in the church, have the power of consecrating and celebrating the Body of Christ. The priest indeed is the minister of God, using the Word of God by God's command and institution; nevertheless God is there the principal Author and invisible Worker, that to whom all that He willeth is subject, and all He commandeth is obedient.

2. Therefore thou must believe God Almighty in this most excellent Sacrament, more than thine own sense or any visible sign at all. And therefore with fear and reverence is this work to be approached. Take heed therefore and see what it is of which the ministry is committed to thee by the laying on of the Bishop's hand. Behold thou art made a priest and art consecrated to celebrate. See now that thou do it before God faithfully and devoutly at due time, and shew thyself without blame. Thou hast not lightened thy burden, but art now bound with a straiter bond of discipline, and art pledged to a higher degree of holiness. A priest ought to be adorned with all virtues and to afford to others an example of good life. His conversation must not be with the popular and common ways of men, but with Angels in Heaven or with perfect men on earth.

3. A priest clad in holy garments taketh Christ's place that he may pray unto God with all supplication and humility for himself and for the whole people. He must always remember the Passion of Christ. He must diligently look upon Christ's footsteps and fervently endeavour himself to follow them. He must bear meekly for God whatsoever ills are brought upon him by others. He must mourn for his own sins, and for the sins committed by others, and

may not grow careless of prayer and holy oblation, until he prevail to obtain grace and mercy. When the priest celebrateth, he honoureth God, giveth joy to the Angels, buildeth up the Church, helpeth the living, hath communion with the departed, and maketh himself a partaker of all good things.

CHAPTER VI

An inquiry concerning preparation for Communion

The Voice of the Disciple

When I consider Thy dignity, O Lord, and mine own vileness, I tremble very exceedingly, and am confounded within myself. For if I approach not, I fly from life; and if I intrude myself unworthily, I run into Thy displeasure. What then shall I do, O my God, Thou helper and Counsellor in necessities.

2. Teach Thou me the right way; propound unto me some short exercise befitting Holy Communion. For it is profitable to know how I ought to prepare my heart devoutly and reverently for Thee, to the intent that I may receive Thy Sacrament to my soul's health [or it may be also for the celebrating this so great and divine mystery].

CHAPTER VII

Of the examination of conscience, and purpose of amendment

The Voice of the Beloved

Above all things the priest of God must draw nigh, with all humility of heart and supplicating reverence, with full faith and pious desire for the honour of God, to celebrate, minister, and receive this Sacrament. Diligently examine thy conscience and with all thy might with true contrition and humble confession cleanse and purify it, so that thou mayest feel no burden, nor know anything which bringeth thee remorse and impedeth thy free approach. Have displeasure against all thy sins in general, and specially sorrow and mourn because of thy daily transgressions. And if thou have time, confess unto God in the secret of thine heart, all miseries of thine own passion.

2. Lament grievously and be sorry, because thou art still so carnal and worldly, so unmortified from thy passions, so full of the motion of concupiscence, so unguarded in thine outward senses, so often entangled in many vain fancies, so much inclined to outward things, so negligent of internal; so ready to laughter and dissoluteness, so unready to weeping and contrition; so prone to ease and indulgence of the flesh, so dull to zeal and fervour; so curious to hear novelties and behold beauties, so loth to embrace things humble and despised; so desirous to have many things, so grudging in giving, so close in keeping; so inconsiderate in speaking, so reluctant to keep silence; so disorderly in manners, so inconsiderate in actions; so eager after food, so deaf towards the Word of God; so eager after rest, so slow to labour; so watchful after tales, so sleepy towards holy watchings; so eager for the end of them, so wandering in attention to them; so negligent in observing the hours of prayer, so lukewarm in celebrating, so unfruitful in communicating; so quickly distracted, so seldom quite collected with thyself; so quickly moved to anger, so ready for displeasure at others; so prone to judging, so severe at reproving; so joyful in prosperity, so weak in adversity; so often making many good resolutions and bringing them to so little effect.

3. When thou hast confessed and bewailed these and thy other shortcomings, with sorrow and sore displeasure at thine own infirmity, make then a firm resolution of continual amendment of life and of progress in all that is good. Then moreover with full resignation and entire will offer thyself to the honour of My name on the altar of thine heart as a perpetual whole burnt-offering, even by faithfully presenting thy body and soul unto Me, to the end that thou mayest so be accounted worthy to draw near to offer this sacrifice of praise and thanksgiving to God, and to receive the Sacrament of My Body and Blood to thy soul's health. For there is no oblation worthier, no satisfaction greater for the destroying of sin, than that a man offer himself to God purely and entirely with the oblation of the Body and Blood of Christ in the Holy Communion. If a man

shall have done what in him lieth, and shall repent him truly, then how often soever he shall draw nigh unto Me for pardon and grace, As I live, saith the Lord, I have no pleasure in the death of a sinner, but rather that he should be converted, and live. All his transgressions that he hath committed, they shall not be mentioned unto him.(1)

(1) Ezekiel xviii. 22, 23.

CHAPTER VIII

Of the oblation of Christ upon the cross, and of resignation of self

The Voice of the Beloved

As I of my own will offered myself unto God the Father on the Cross for thy sins with outstretched hands and naked body, so that nothing remained in Me that did not become altogether a sacrifice for the Divine propitiation; so also oughtest thou every day to offer thyself willingly unto Me for a pure and holy oblation with all thy strength and affections, even to the utmost powers of thine heart. What more do I require of thee than thou study to resign thyself altogether unto Me? Whatsoever thou givest besides thyself, I nothing care for, for I ask not thy gift, but thee.

2. As it would not be sufficient for thee if thou hadst all things except Me, even so whatsoever thou shalt give Me, if thou give Me not thyself, it cannot please Me. Offer thyself to Me, and give thyself altogether for God, so shall thy offering be accepted. Behold I offered Myself altogether to the Father for thee, I give also My whole body and blood for food, that thou mightest remain altogether Mine and I thine. But if thou stand in thyself, and offer not thyself freely to My will, thy offering is not perfect, neither shall the union betwixt us be complete. Therefore ought the freewill offering of thyself into the hands of God to go before all thy works, if thou wilt attain liberty and grace. For this is the cause that so few are inwardly enlightened and made free, that they know not how to deny

themselves entirely. My word standeth sure, Except a man forsake all, he cannot be My disciple.(1) Thou therefore, if thou wilt be My disciple, offer thyself to Me with all thy affections.

(1) Luke xiv. 33.

CHAPTER IX

That we ought to offer ourselves and all that is ours to God, and to pray for all

The Voice of the Disciple

Lord, all that is in the heaven and in the earth is Thine.(1) I desire to offer myself up unto thee as a freewill offering, and to continue Thine for ever. Lord, in the uprightness of mine heart I willingly offer(2) myself to Thee to-day to be Thy servant for ever, in humble submission and for a sacrifice of perpetual praise. Receive me with this holy Communion of Thy precious Body, which I celebrate before Thee this day in the presence of the Angels invisibly surrounding, that it may be for the salvation of me and of all Thy people.

2. Lord, I lay before Thee at this celebration all my sins and offences which I have committed before Thee and Thy holy Angels, from the day whereon I was first able to sin even unto this hour; that Thou mayest consume and burn them every one with the fire of Thy charity, and mayest do away all the stains of my sins, and cleanse my conscience from all offence, and restore me to Thy favour which by sinning I have lost, fully forgiving me all, and mercifully admitting me to the kiss of peace.

3. What can I do concerning my sins, save humbly to confess and lament them and unceasingly to beseech Thy propitiation? I beseech Thee, be propitious unto me and hear me, when I stand before Thee, O my God. All my sins displease me grievously: I will never more commit them; but I grieve for them and will grieve so long as I live, steadfastly purposing to repent me truly, and to make restitution as far as I can. Forgive, O God, forgive me my sins for Thy holy Name's sake; save my soul, which Thou hast

redeemed with Thy precious blood. Behold I commit myself to Thy mercy, I resign myself to Thy hands. Deal with me according to Thy loving-kindness, not according to my wickedness and iniquity.

4. I offer also unto Thee all my goodness, though it is exceedingly little and imperfect, that Thou mayest mend and sanctify it, that Thou mayest make it well pleasing and acceptable in Thy sight, and ever draw it on towards perfection; and furthermore bring me safely, slothful and useless poor creature that I am, to a happy and blessed end.

5. Moreover I offer unto Thee all pious desires of the devout, necessities of parents, friends, brothers, sisters, and all who are dear to me, and of those who have done good to me, or to others for Thy love; and those who have desired and besought my prayers for themselves and all belonging to them; that all may feel themselves assisted by Thy grace, enriched by consolation, protected from dangers, freed from pains; and that being delivered from all evils they may joyfully give Thee exceeding thanks.

6. I offer also to Thee prayers and Sacramental intercessions for those specially who have injured me in aught, made me sad, or spoken evil concerning me, or have caused me any loss or displeasure; for all those also whom I have at any time made sad, disturbed, burdened, and scandalized, by words or deeds, knowingly or ignorantly; that to all of us alike, Thou mayest equally pardon our sins and mutual offences. Take away, O Lord, from our hearts all suspicion, indignation, anger, and contention, and whatsoever is able to injure charity and diminish brotherly love. Have mercy, have mercy, Lord, on those who entreat Thy mercy; give grace to the needy; and make us such that we may be worthy to enjoy Thy grace, and go forward to the life eternal. Amen.

(1) 1 Chronicles xxix. 11.   (2) 1 Chronicles xxix. 17.

CHAPTER X

That Holy Communion is not lightly to be omitted

The Voice of the Beloved

Thou must frequently betake thee to the Fountain of grace and divine mercy, to the Fountain of goodness and all purity; to the end that thou mayest obtain the healing of thy passions and vices, and mayest be made stronger and more watchful against all temptations and wiles of the devil. The enemy, knowing what profit and exceeding strong remedy lieth in the Holy Communion, striveth by all means and occasions to draw back and hinder the faithful and devout, so far as he can.

2. For when some set about to prepare themselves for Holy Communion, they suffer from the more evil suggestions of Satan. The very evil spirit himself (as is written in Job), cometh among the sons of God that he may trouble them by his accustomed evil dealing, or make them over timid and perplexed; to the intent that he may diminish their affections, or take away their faith by his attacks, if haply he may prevail upon them to give up Holy Communion altogether, or to come thereto with lukewarm hearts. But his wiles and delusions must not be heeded, howsoever wicked and terrible they be; but all his delusion must be cast back upon his own head. The wretch must be despised and laughed to scorn: neither must Holy Communion be omitted because of his insults and the inward troubles which he stirreth up.

3. Often also too much carefulness or some anxiety or other touching confession hindereth from obtaining devotion. Do thou according to the counsel of wise men, and lay aside anxiety and scruple, because it hindereth the grace of God and destroyeth devotion of mind. Because of some little vexation or trouble do not thou neglect Holy Communion, but rather hasten to confess it, and forgive freely all offences committed against thee. And if thou hast offended any man, humbly beg for pardon, and God shall freely forgive thee.

4. What profiteth it to put off for long time the confession of thy sins, or to defer Holy Communion? Cleanse thyself forthwith,

spit out the poison with all speed, hasten to take the remedy, and thou shalt feel thyself better than if thou didst long defer it. If to-day thou defer it on one account, to-morrow perchance some greater obstacle will come, and so thou mayest be long time hindered from Communion and become more unfit. As soon as thou canst, shake thyself from thy present heaviness and sloth, for it profiteth nothing to be long anxious, to go long on thy way with heaviness of heart, and because of daily little obstacles to sever thyself from divine things: nay it is exceeding hurtful to defer thy Communion long, for this commonly bringeth on great torpor. Alas! there are some, lukewarm and undisciplined, who willingly find excuses for delaying repentance, and desire to defer Holy Communion, lest they should be bound to keep stricter watch upon themselves.

5. Alas! how little charity, what flagging devotion, have they who so lightly put off Holy Communion. How happy is he, how acceptable to God, who so liveth, and in such purity of conscience keepeth himself, that any day he could be ready and well inclined to communicate, if it were in his power, and might be done without the notice of others. If a man sometimes abstaineth for the sake of humility or some sound cause, he is to be commended for his reverence. But if drowsiness have taken hold of him, he ought to rouse himself and to do what in him lieth; and the Lord will help his desire for the good will which he hath, which God specially approveth.

6. But when he is hindered by sufficient cause, yet will he ever have a good will and pious intention to communicate; and so he shall not be lacking in the fruit of the Sacrament. For any devout man is able every day and every hour to draw near to spiritual communion with Christ to his soul's health and without hindrance. Nevertheless on certain days and at the appointed time he ought to receive the Body and Blood of his Redeemer with affectionate reverence, and rather to seek after the praise and honour of God, than his own comfort. For so often doth he communicate mystically, and is invisibly refreshed, as he devoutly calleth to mind the mystery of Christ's incarnation and His Passion, and is inflamed with the love of Him.

7. He who only prepareth himself when a festival is at hand or

custom compelleth, will too often be unprepared. Blessed is he who offereth himself to God for a whole burnt-offering, so often as he celebrateth or communicateth! Be not too slow nor too hurried in thy celebrating, but preserve the good received custom of those with whom thou livest. Thou oughtest not to produce weariness and annoyance in others, but to observe the received custom, according to the institution of the elders; and to minister to the profit of others rather than to thine own devotion or feeling.

CHAPTER XI

That the Body and Blood of Christ and the Holy Scriptures are most necessary to a faithful soul

The Voice of the Disciple

O most sweet Lord Jesus, how great is the blessedness of the devout soul that feedeth with Thee in Thy banquet, where there is set before it no other food than Thyself its only Beloved, more to be desired than all the desires of the heart? And to me it would verily be sweet to pour forth my tears in Thy presence from the very bottom of my heart, and with the pious Magdalene to water Thy feet with my tears. But where is this devotion? Where the abundant flowing of holy tears? Surely in Thy presence and in the presence of the holy Angels my whole heart ought to burn and to weep for joy; for I have Thee in the Sacrament verily present, although hidden under other form.

2. For in Thine own Divine brightness, mine eyes could not endure to behold Thee, neither could the whole world stand before the splendour of the glory of Thy Majesty. In this therefore Thou hast consideration unto my weakness, that Thou hidest Thyself under the Sacrament. I verily possess and adore Him whom the Angels adore in heaven; I yet for a while by faith, but they by sight and without a veil. It is good for me to be content with the light of true faith, and to walk therein until the day of eternal brightness dawn, and the shadows of figures flee away.(1) But when that which is perfect is come, the using of Sacraments shall cease, because the Blessed in heavenly glory have no need

of Sacramental remedy. For they rejoice unceasingly in the presence of God, beholding His glory face to face, and being changed from glory to glory(2) of the infinite God, they taste the Word of God made flesh, as He was in the beginning and remaineth for everlasting.

3. When I think on these wondrous things, even spiritual comfort whatsoever it be becometh sore weariness to me; for so long as I see not openly my Lord in His own Glory, I count for nothing all which I behold and hear in the world. Thou, O God, art my witness that nothing is able to comfort me, no creature is able to give me rest, save Thou, O my God, whom I desire to contemplate everlastingly. But this is not possible, so long as I remain in this mortal state. Therefore ought I to set myself unto great patience, and submit myself unto Thee in every desire. For even Thy Saints, O Lord, who now rejoice with Thee in the kingdom of heaven, waited for the coming of Thy glory whilst they lived here, in faith and great glory. What they believed, that believe I; what they hoped, I hope; whither they have attained to, thither through Thy grace hope I to come. I will walk meanwhile in faith, strengthened by the examples of the Saints. I will have also holy books for comfort and for a mirror of life, and above them all Thy most holy Body and Blood shall be for me a special remedy and refuge.

4. For two things do I feel to be exceedingly necessary to me in this life, without which this miserable life would be intolerable to me; being detained in the prison of this body, I confess that I need two things, even food and light. Thou hast therefore given to me who am so weak, Thy sacred Body and Blood, for the refreshing of my soul and body, and hast set Thy Word for a lantern to my feet.(3) Without these two I could not properly live; for the Word of God is the light of my soul, and Thy Sacrament the bread of life. These may also be called the two tables, placed on this side and on that, in the treasury of Thy holy Church. One table is that of the Sacred Altar, bearing the holy bread, that is the precious Body and Blood of Christ; the other is the table of the Divine Law, containing holy doctrine, teaching the true faith, and leading steadfastly onwards even to that which is within the veil, where the Holy of Holies is.

5. Thanks be unto Thee, O Lord Jesus, Light of Light everlasting, for that table of holy doctrine which Thou has furnished unto us by Thy servants the Prophets and Apostles and other teachers. Thanks be to Thee, O Creator and Redeemer of men, who to make known Thy love to the whole world has prepared a great supper, in which Thou hast set forth for good not the typical lamb, but Thine own most Holy Body and Blood; making all Thy faithful ones joyful with this holy banquet and giving them to drink the cup of salvation, wherein are all the delights of Paradise, and the holy Angels do feed with us, and with yet happier sweetness.

6. Oh how great and honourable is the office of the priests, to whom it is given to consecrate the Sacrament of the Lord of majesty with holy words, to bless it with the lips, to hold it in their hands, to receive it with their own mouth, and to administer it to others! Oh how clean ought those hands to be, how pure the mouth, how holy the body, how unspotted the heart of the priest, to whom so often the Author of purity entereth in! From the mouth of the priest ought naught to proceed but what is holy, what is honest and profitable, because he so often receiveth the Sacrament of Christ.

7. His eyes ought to be single and pure, seeing they are wont to look upon the Body of Christ; the hands should be pure and lifted towards heaven, which are wont to hold within them the Creator of heaven and earth. To priests is it specially said in the Law, Be ye holy, for I the Lord your God am holy.(4)

8. Assist us with Thy grace, O Almighty God, that we who have taken upon us the priestly office, may be able to converse worthily and devoutly with Thee in all purity and good conscience. And if we are not able to have our conversation in such innocency of life as we ought, yet grant unto us worthily to lament the sins which we have committed, and in the spirit of humility and full purpose of a good will, to serve Thee more earnestly for the future.

(1) Cant. ii. 17.   (2) 2 Corinthians iii. 18.
(3) Psalm cxix. 105.   (4) Leviticus xix. 2.

CHAPTER XII

That he who is about to Communicate with Christ ought to prepare himself with great diligence

The Voice of the Beloved

I am the Lover of purity, and Giver of sanctity. I seek a pure heart, and there is the place of My rest. Prepare for Me the larger upper room furnished, and I will keep the Passover at thy house with my disciples.(1) If thou wilt that I come unto thee and abide with thee, purge out the old leaven,(2) and cleanse the habitation of thy heart. Shut out the whole world, and all the throng of sins; sit as a sparrow alone upon the house-top,(3) and think upon thy transgressions with bitterness of thy soul. For everyone that loveth prepareth the best and fairest place for his beloved, because hereby the affection of him that entertaineth his beloved is known.

2. Yet know thou that thou canst not make sufficient preparation out of the merit of any action of thine, even though thou shouldest prepare thyself for a whole year, and hadst nothing else in thy mind. But out of My tenderness and grace alone art thou permitted to draw nigh unto My table; as though a beggar were called to a rich man's dinner, and had no other recompense to offer him for the benefits done unto him, but to humble himself and to give him thanks. Do therefore as much as lieth in thee, and do it diligently, not of custom, nor of necessity, but with fear, reverence, and affection, receive the Body of thy beloved Lord God, who vouchsafeth to come unto thee. I am He who hath called thee; I commanded it to be done; I will supply what is lacking to thee; come and receive Me.

3. When I give the grace of devotion, give thanks unto thy God; it is not because thou art worthy, but because I had mercy on thee. If thou hast not devotion, but rather feelest thyself dry, be instant in prayer, cease not to groan and knock; cease not until thou prevail to obtain some crumb or drop of saving grace. Thou hast need of Me, I have no need of thee. Nor dost thou come to sanctify Me, but I come to sanctify thee and make thee better. Thou comest that thou mayest be sanctified by Me, and be united

to Me; that thou mayest receive fresh grace, and be kindled anew to amendment of life. See that thou neglect not this grace, but prepare thy heart with all diligence, and receive thy Beloved unto thee.

4. But thou oughtest not only to prepare thyself for devotion before Communion, thou must also keep thyself with all diligence therein after receiving the Sacrament; nor is less watchfulness needed afterwards, than devout preparation beforehand: for good watchfulness afterwards becometh in turn the best preparation for the gaining more grace. For hereby is a man made entirely indisposed to good, if he immediately return from Communion to give himself up to outward consolations. Beware of much speaking; remain in a secret place, and hold communion with thy God; for thou hast Him whom the whole world cannot take away from thee. I am He to whom thou oughtest wholly to give thyself; so that now thou mayest live not wholly in thyself, but in Me, free from all anxiety.

(1) Mark xiv. 14, 15. (2) 1 Corinthians v. 7.
(3) Psalm cii. 7.

CHAPTER XIII

That the devout soul ought with the whole heart to yearn after union with Christ in the Sacrament

The Voice of the Disciple

Who shall grant unto me, O Lord, that I may find Thee alone, and open all my heart unto Thee, and enjoy Thee as much as my soul desireth; and that no man may henceforth look upon me, nor any creature move me or have respect unto me, but Thou alone speak unto me and I unto Thee, even as beloved is wont to speak unto beloved, and friend to feast with friend? For this do I pray, this do I long for, that I may be wholly united unto Thee, and may withdraw my heart from all created things, and by means of Holy Communion and frequent celebration may learn more and more to relish heavenly and eternal things. Ah, Lord God, when shall I be entirely united and lost in Thee, and altogether forgetful of myself? Thou in me, and I in Thee;(1) even so grant that we may in like manner continue together in one.

2. Verily Thou art my Beloved, the choicest among ten thousand,(2) in whom my soul delighteth to dwell all the days of her life. Verily Thou art my Peacemaker, in Whom is perfect peace and true rest, apart from Whom is labour and sorrow and infinite misery. Verily Thou art a God that hidest Thyself, and Thy counsel is not with the wicked, but Thy Word is with the humble and the simple. O how sweet, O Lord, is Thy spirit, who that Thou mightest manifest Thy sweetness towards Thy children, dost vouchsafe to refresh them with the bread which is full of sweetness, which cometh down from heaven. Verily there is no other nation so great, which hath its gods drawing nigh to them, as Thou, our God, art present unto all Thy faithful ones,(3) unto whom for their daily solace, and for lifting up their heart unto heaven, Thou givest Thyself for their food and delight.

3. For what other nation is there so renowned as the Christian people? Or what creature is so beloved under heaven as the devout soul to which God entereth in, that he may feed it with His glorious flesh? O unspeakable grace! O wonderful condescension! O immeasurable love specially bestowed upon men! But what reward shall I give unto the Lord for this grace, for charity so mighty? There is nothing which I am able to present more acceptable than to give my heart altogether unto God, and to join it inwardly to Him. Then all my inward parts shall rejoice, when my soul shall be perfectly united unto God. Then shall He say unto me, "If thou wilt be with Me, I will be with thee." And I will answer Him, "Vouchsafe, O Lord, to abide with me, I will gladly be with Thee; this is my whole desire, even that my heart be united unto Thee."

(1) John xv. 4.   (2) Cant. v. 10.   (3) Deuteronomy iv. 7.

CHAPTER XIV

Of the fervent desire of certain devout persons to receive the Body and Blood of Christ

The Voice of the Disciple

O how great is the abundance of Thy sweetness, O Lord, which Thou hast laid up for them that fear Thee. When I call to mind some devout persons who draw nigh to Thy Sacrament, O Lord, with the deepest devotion and affection, then very often I am confounded in myself and blush for shame, that I approach Thine altar and table of Holy Communion so carelessly and coldly, that I remain so dry and without affection, that I am not wholly kindled with love before Thee, my God, nor so vehemently drawn and affected as many devout persons have been, who out of the very earnest desire of the Communion, and tender affection of heart, could not refrain from weeping, but as it were with mouth of heart and body alike panted inwardly after Thee, O God, O Fountain of Life, having no power to appease or satiate their hunger, save by receiving Thy Body with all joyfulness and spiritual eagerness.

2. O truly ardent faith of those, becoming a very proof of Thy Sacred Presence! For they verily know their Lord in the breaking of bread, whose heart so ardently burneth within them[1] when Jesus walketh with them by the way. Ah me! far from me for the most part is such love and devotion as this, such vehement love and ardour. Be merciful unto me, O Jesus, good, sweet, and kind, and grant unto Thy poor suppliant to feel sometimes, in Holy Communion, though it be but a little, the cordial affection of Thy love, that my faith may grow stronger, my hope in Thy goodness increase, and my charity, once kindled within me by the tasting of the heavenly manna, may never fail.

3. But Thy mercy is able even to grant me the grace which I long for, and to visit me most tenderly with the spirit of fervour when the day of Thy good pleasure shall come. For, although I burn not with desire so vehement as theirs who are specially devout towards Thee, yet, through Thy grace, I have a desire after that greatly inflamed desire, praying and desiring to be made partaker with all those who so fervently love Thee, and to be numbered among their holy company.

[1] Luke xxiv. 32.

CHAPTER XV

That the grace of devotion is acquired by humility and self-denial

The Voice of the Beloved

Thou oughtest to seek earnestly the grace of devotion, to ask it fervently, to wait for it patiently and faithfully, to receive it gratefully, to preserve it humbly, to work with it diligently, and to leave to God the time and manner of heavenly visitation until it come. Chiefly oughtest thou to humble thyself when thou feelest inwardly little or no devotion, yet not to be too much cast down, nor to grieve out of measure. God ofttimes giveth in one short moment what He hath long time denied; He sometimes giveth at the end what at the beginning of prayer He hath deferred to give.

2. If grace were always given immediately, and were at hand at the wish, it would be hardly bearable to weak man. Wherefore the grace of devotion is to be waited for with a good hope and with humble patience. Yet impute it to thyself and to thy sins when it is not given, or when it is mysteriously taken away. It is sometimes a small thing which hindereth and hideth grace; (if indeed that ought to be called small and not rather great, which hindereth so great a good); but if thou remove this, be it small or great, and perfectly overcome it, thou wilt have what thou hast asked.

3. For immediately that thou hast given thyself unto God with all thine heart, and hast sought neither this nor that according to thine own will and pleasure, but hast altogether settled thyself in Him, thou shalt find thyself united and at peace; because nothing shall give thee so sweet relish and delight, as the good pleasure of the Divine will. Whosoever therefore shall have lifted up his will unto God with singleness of heart, and shall have delivered himself from every inordinate love or dislike of any created thing, he will be the most fit for receiving grace, and worthy of the gift of devotion. For where the Lord findeth empty vessels,(1) there giveth He His blessing. And the more perfectly a man forsaketh things which cannot profit, and the

more he dieth to himself, the more quickly doth grace come, the more plentifully doth it enter in, and the higher doth it lift up the free heart.

4. Then shall he see, and flow together, and wonder, and his heart shall be enlarged within him,(2) because the hand of the Lord is with him, and he hath put himself wholly in His hand, even for ever. Lo, thus shall the man be blessed, that seeketh God with all his heart, and receiveth not his soul in vain. This man in receiving the Holy Eucharist obtaineth the great grace of Divine Union; because he hath not regard to his own devotion and comfort, but, above all devotion and comfort, to the glory and honour of God.

(1) 2 Kings iv.   (2) Isaiah lx. 5.

CHAPTER XVI

That we ought to lay open our necessities to Christ and to require His Grace

The Voice of the Disciple

O most sweet and loving Lord, whom now I devoutly desire to receive, Thou knowest my infirmity and the necessity which I suffer, in what evils and vices I lie; how often I am weighed down, tempted, disturbed, and defiled. I come unto Thee for remedy, I beseech of Thee consolation and support. I speak unto Thee who knowest all things, to whom all my secrets are open, and who alone art able perfectly to comfort and help me. Thou knowest what good thing I most stand in need of, and how poor I am in virtues.

2. Behold, I stand poor and naked before Thee, requiring grace, and imploring mercy. Refresh the hungry suppliant, kindle my coldness with the fire of Thy love, illuminate my blindness with the brightness of Thy presence. Turn thou all earthly things into bitterness for me, all grievous and contrary things into patience, all things worthless and created into contempt and oblivion. Lift up my heart unto Thee in Heaven, and suffer me

not to wander over the earth. Be Thou alone sweet unto me from this day forward for ever, because Thou alone art my meat and drink, my love and joy, my sweetness and my whole good.

3. Oh that Thou wouldest altogether by Thy presence, kindle, consume, and transform me into Thyself; that I may be made one spirit with Thee, by the grace of inward union, and the melting of earnest love! Suffer me not to go away from Thee hungry and dry; but deal mercifully with me, as oftentimes Thou hast dealt wondrously with Thy saints. What marvel if I should be wholly kindled from Thee, and in myself should utterly fail, since Thou art fire always burning and never failing, love purifying the heart and enlightening the understanding.

CHAPTER XVII

Of fervent love and vehement desire of receiving Christ

The Voice of the Disciple

With the deepest devotion and fervent love, with all affection and fervour of heart, I long to receive Thee, O Lord, even as many Saints and devout persons have desired Thee in communicating, who were altogether well pleasing to Thee by their sanctity of life, and dwelt in all ardent devotion. O my God, Eternal Love, my whole Good, Happiness without measure, I long to receive Thee with the most vehement desire and becoming reverence which any Saint ever had or could have.

2. And although I be unworthy to have all those feelings of devotion, yet do I offer Thee the whole affection of my heart, even as though I alone had all those most grateful inflamed desires. Yea, also, whatsoever things a pious mind is able to conceive and long for, all these with the deepest veneration and inward fervour do I offer and present unto Thee. I desire to reserve nothing unto myself, but freely and entirely to offer myself and all that I have unto Thee for a sacrifice. O Lord my God, my Creator and Redeemer! with such affection, reverence, praise, and honour, with such gratitude, worthiness, and love, with such faith, hope, and purity do I desire to receive Thee

this day, as Thy most blessed Mother, the glorious Virgin Mary, received and desired Thee, when she humbly and devoutly answered the Angel who brought unto her the glad tidings of the mystery of the Incarnation. Behold the handmaid of the Lord; be it unto me according to thy word.(1)

3. And as Thy blessed forerunner, the most excellent of Saints, John Baptist, being full of joy in Thy presence, leapt while yet in the womb of his mother, for joy in the Holy Ghost; and afterwards discerning Jesus walking amongst men, humbled himself exceedingly, and said, with devout affection, The friend of the bridegroom, who standeth and heareth him, rejoiceth greatly because of the bridegroom's voice;(2) even so I wish to be inflamed with great and holy desires, and to present myself unto Thee with my whole heart. Whence also, on behalf of myself and of all commended to me in prayer, I offer and present unto Thee the jubilation of all devout hearts, their ardent affections, their mental ecstasies, and supernatural illuminations and heavenly visions, with all the virtues and praises celebrated and to be celebrated by every creature in heaven and earth; to the end that by all Thou mayest worthily be praised and glorified for ever.

4. Receive my prayers, O Lord my God, and my desires of giving Thee infinite praise and unbounded benediction, which, according to the multitude of Thine unspeakable greatness, are most justly due unto Thee. These do I give Thee, and desire to give every day and every moment; and with beseechings and affectionate desires I call upon all celestial spirits and all Thy faithful people to join with me in rendering Thee thanks and praises.

5. Let all peoples, nations, and tongues praise Thee, and magnify Thy holy and sweet-sounding Name, with highest jubilations and ardent devotion. And let all who reverently and devoutly celebrate Thy most high Sacrament, and receive it with full assurance of faith, be accounted worthy to find grace and mercy with Thee, and intercede with all supplication for me a sinner; and when they shall have attained unto their wished-for devotion and joyous union with Thee, and shall depart full of comfort and wondrously refreshed from Thy holy, heavenly table, let them vouchsafe to be mindful of me, for I am poor and needy.

(1) Luke i. 38. (2) John iii. 29.

CHAPTER XVIII

That a man should not be a curious searcher of the Sacrament, but a humble imitator of Christ, submitting his sense to holy faith

The Voice of the Beloved

Thou must take heed of curious and useless searching into this most profound Sacrament, if thou wilt not be plunged into the abyss of doubt. He that is a searcher of Majesty shall be oppressed by the glory thereof.(1) God is able to do more than man can understand. A pious and humble search after truth is to be allowed, when it is always ready to be taught, and striving to walk after the wholesome opinions of the fathers.

2. Blessed is the simplicity which leaveth alone the difficult paths of questionings, and followeth the plain and firm steps of God's commandments. Many have lost devotion whilst they sought to search into deeper things. Faith is required of thee, and a sincere life, not loftiness of intellect, nor deepness in the mysteries of God. If thou understandest not nor comprehendest the things which are beneath thee, how shalt thou comprehend those which are above thee? Submit thyself unto God, and humble thy sense to faith, and the light of knowledge shall be given thee, as shall be profitable and necessary unto thee.

3. There are some who are grievously tempted concerning faith and the Sacrament; but this is not to be imputed to themselves but rather to the enemy. Care not then for this, dispute not with thine own thoughts, nor make answer to the doubts which are cast into thee by the devil; but believe the words of God, believe His Saints and Prophets, and the wicked enemy shall flee from thee. Often it profiteth much, that the servant of God endureth such things. For the enemy tempteth not unbelievers and sinners, because he already hath secure possession of them; but he tempteth and harasseth the faithful and devout by various means.

4. Go forward therefore with simple and undoubting faith, and draw nigh unto the Sacrament with supplicating reverence. And whatsoever thou art not enabled to understand, that commit without anxiety to Almighty God. God deceiveth thee not; he is deceived who believeth too much in himself. God walketh with the simple, revealeth Himself to the humble, giveth understanding to babes, openeth the sense to pure minds, and hideth grace from the curious and proud. Human reason is weak and may be deceived; but true faith cannot be deceived.

5. All reason and natural investigation ought to follow faith, not to precede, nor to break it. For faith and love do here especially take the highest place, and work in hidden ways in this most holy and exceeding excellent Sacrament. God who is eternal and incomprehensible, and of infinite power, doth great and inscrutable things in heaven and in earth, and His wonderful works are past finding out. If the works of God were of such sort that they might easily be comprehended by human reason, they should no longer be called wonderful or unspeakable.

(1) Proverbs xxv. 27 (Vulg.).

Printed in Great Britain
by Amazon